A CIVIC SPIRITUALITY OF SANCTIFICATION

Past Light on Present Life:
Theology, Ethics, and Spirituality

Roger Haight, SJ, Alfred Pach III,
and *Amanda Avila Kaminski,* series editors

These volumes are offered to the academic community of teachers and learners in the fields of Christian history, theology, ethics, and spirituality. They introduce classic texts by authors whose contributions have markedly affected the development of Christianity, especially in the West. The texts are accompanied by an introductory essay on context and key themes and followed by an interpretation that dialogically engages the original message with the issues of ethics, theology, and spirituality in the present.

A Civic Spirituality of Sanctification

JOHN CALVIN

EDITED AND WITH COMMENTARY BY
*Roger Haight, SJ, Alfred Pach III,
and Amanda Avila Kaminski*

FORDHAM UNIVERSITY PRESS   NEW YORK 2024

This series has been generously supported by a theological education grant from the E. Rhodes and Leona B. Carpenter Foundation.

Selections from Calvin's Institutes of the Christian Religion are reprinted from John T. McNeil, ed., Ford Lewis Battles, trans., *Calvin: Institutes of the Christian Religion* (Philadelphia: The Westminster Press, 1960), 356–65, 597–603, and 684–725. Used with permission.

Fordham University Press has no responsibility for the persistence or accuracy of URLs for external or third-party Internet websites referred to in this publication and does not guarantee that any content on such websites is, or will remain, accurate or appropriate.

Fordham University Press also publishes its books in a variety of electronic formats. Some content that appears in print may not be available in electronic books.

Visit us online at www.fordhampress.com.

Library of Congress Cataloging-in-Publication Data available online at https://catalog.loc.gov.

Printed in the United States of America

26 25 24   5 4 3 2 1

First edition

Contents

A CIVIC SPIRITUALITY OF SANCTIFICATION

I

Introduction to Calvin and the Texts

The German sociologist of religion Ernst Troeltsch suggested that it has been at two points only that Christianity has been able to decisively transform human culture and civilization: during the Middle Ages, through the scholastic synthesis of Thomas Aquinas, and in the early modern period, through Calvinism. To engage with Calvin and his legacy is thus to wrestle with one of the rare moments in modern history when Christianity molded, rather than accommodated itself to, society.[1]

Calvin did not write an autobiography or memoir. And yet his formation and the subsequent events in his life explain or at least situate his legacy and help us understand it. In the case of some figures, one event in the whole story explains everything. In others, a single deep idea represents the key that will open up the world within. Calvin requires a series of events and a set of keys because several doors open to the world of his thought and the spirituality that accompanies it.

This Introduction begins with the temporal stages of Calvin's formation, for they are major pieces of the puzzle. It then offers a précis of his intellectual world in a list of factors that

3

help to describe this reformer, each of which could serve as a starting point for organizing the crowd of ideas that Calvin represents. It concludes by describing the texts and how they relate to one another in terms of their content. This will supply an outline for reading Calvin. The texts do not capture the full range of Calvin's spirituality, but they provide a foundation for his brilliant "alliance between religious thought and action."[2]

John Calvin

John Calvin was born Jehan or Jean Cauvin in Noyon, a relatively small cathedral city in Picardy, a region north of Paris, in 1509. His father worked as an accountant for the cathedral and was able to secure the funds to send his talented son to the University of Paris at the age of fourteen. Not long afterward, he was enrolled in the prestigious Collège de Montaigu. He was destined to study theology. However, early in 1528, at eighteen, he ended his studies in Paris and, at the behest of his father, moved to Orléans to pursue a degree in law. Calvin interrupted his study in Orléans for a time at Bourges, but "in 1531, Calvin graduated as *licencié ès lois* from the University of Orléans."[3]

Calvin underwent major transitions during the years from 1531 to 1536. In 1531, his father succumbed to illness, and the fact that he could not negotiate his father's release from an excommunication because of a financial conflict with the cathedral surely affected his relation to the church. Having finished his law studies, Calvin turned his attention to his new passion, the study of ancient literature, and in 1532 published a critical text of Seneca's De Clementia. In the fall of 1533, he was in Paris when his friend Nicholas Cop, the new rector of the University of Paris, delivered an address that so favored positions associated with the reform movement that he (Cop) had to flee the city. Calvin, the newly born humanist, also left the city, because he was known to be sympathetic to the ideas of reform. He spent the winter of 1533–34 with another friend, the parish priest in Claix, outside Angoulême, who had a substantial library. Calvin used the time to read theology. It is likely that during this period Calvin fully embraced the evangelical movement, because in the spring he surrendered hope of reform from within and gave up his benefices to the Canons of the cathedral of Noyons. In two separate paragraphs of his writings, Calvin gives a brief account of his conversion: In the light of scripture, he could no longer accept the authority structure and teachings of the Catholic Church. Calvin then set out to compose between 1534 and 1535 a basic statement of the evangelical faith that he called the *Institutes of the Christian Religion*.[4] It was published in the spring of 1536 and immediately established Calvin as a notable reformation theologian. He was twenty-seven years old.

In 1536, Calvin resolved to move to Strasbourg and commit himself to scholarship. Because of local wars, his journey there had to be detoured to the south, and he passed through Geneva. When Guillaume (William) Farel, the leading reformer in the city, learned of Calvin's arrival in the city, he encountered him and convinced him to stay and organize the church in the city. He began this work in August 1536. His aggressive measures, however, were terminated within two years mainly for reasons associated with Geneva's political factions. Thus, from 1538 to 1541 Calvin pastored a reformed church in Strasbourg, where he learned in a hands-on way how to lead a congregation. Finally, in 1541, Calvin took the step that would launch his life's work. As the tumultuous religious situation in Geneva finally reached a critical point, the city magistrates asked Calvin to return after having failed to convince him to do so a year earlier. In September, he moved to Geneva for good. He was thirty-two and carried massive credentials to the task of creating a Christian church. He had been educated at the University of Paris, and he was a lawyer, a published Renaissance scholar, an experienced pastor, and a recognized reformed theologian. He worked at shaping the church at Geneva for almost twenty more years. His last years were quiet, and he died in 1564.

Distinguishing Features of Calvin's Theology

As a second-generation reformer, Calvin built his project on principal ideas and doctrines of Luther. The *Institutes* of 1536 even used the outline of Luther's Small Catechism and borrowed from his theology. Like Luther before him, Calvin insisted on homilies' and songs' being preached and sung in the language spoken by the local people in order to ensure the participation, understanding, and edification of the congregation. This background makes it important to trace the roots of the distinctiveness of Calvin, the church he inspired, and especially the contours of his spirituality.[5] What follows describes some of those differentiating factors in order to highlight features that, when they are held together, help define the uniqueness of Calvin's spirituality. The items operate as distinctively colored threads in the fabric of his thinking. Each one describes an important circumstance or feature of Calvin's vision. Together they form a perspective for this representation and interpretation of Calvin's spirituality.

Geneva. Major contours of Calvin's spirituality take shape in response to the realities of his work in Geneva. He had to adapt to the city and contend with major theological critiques, much political jockeying, and significant conflict as he developed a reformation spirituality that is ecclesial throughout. Geneva was an autonomous city-state or republic that had just won its independence from a prince-bishop shortly before Calvin arrived.[6] It was governed by the citizens through a series of councils or assemblies with four officials at the top who were the chief magistrates. They met three times a week with the Small Council, which administered the city. Behind them was a larger Council of Sixty, a Council of Two-Hundred, and a General Assembly of the male citizens of Geneva that met twice a year. Each had assigned tasks; the General Assembly elected the four chief magistrates or "Syndics." This city government had gradually edged out the prince-bishop and voted to accept the Reformation. It was wary of religious authority, having just won its independence, and Calvin had to design the church that fitted this city. After his return, a symbiotic relationship, not without some severe tensions, between Calvin's ecclesiology, spirituality, and Geneva would gradually emerge, but it took years.

Integration. Calvin was an organizer. He had a tidy mind. This quality and ability permeated his work and was displayed at several levels. He organized the church in Geneva, beginning with founding documents, and then developed the theology around them.[7] He helped to write Geneva's constitution. As a theologian, he wrote what was in effect a systematic theology that stands out in the whole history of Christianity. His theological conceptions and his actions consistently informed each other. An overall internal logic governed Calvin's thinking. In fact, he added system and organization to the reformation movement. This organizational cast of mind was not airy but commonsensical and directed toward concrete behavior. Calvin's writing drew from scripture and used the traditional language and concepts of the discipline. But his spirituality extended to concrete behavior; ethics and theology were hand in glove, so that spirituality related one to God and elicited specific moral norms. His ecclesiology included oversight of behavior in the churches of the city and its environs. Integrity in Calvin points to a coherence of thought within a wide horizon of vision and concrete behavioral norms.

Sovereignty of God. It would be difficult to overestimate the awesome sovereignty of God in Calvin's imagination. Like Luther, Calvin was impressed by the absolute transcendence of God who is wholly other. But while the awesomeness of God was softened in Luther by God's Word of love in Christ, Calvin dwells on the majesty, glory, and absolute power of

God. Of course, all Christian spirituality shares some Christ-centeredness. Creator God cannot be said to minimize the centrality of Christ to Christian spirituality. But Calvin situates Christ within the context of the sovereign glory of God. All things transpire within and in accord with the transcendent oversight of God. Theocentrism draws an outer circle around Calvin's Christocentrism.

God's Will. God's sovereignty involves God's will; it brings God's power to a focal point. The idea of God's absolute will suffuses all of Calvin's thought. God's commanding will acts in God's creation and governance of the world. Calvin is probably most famous for his preservation of Augustine's view of providence and predestination. Troeltsch dwells on Calvin's insistence on God's predestination of all things; every event and outcome has been decided within God's oversight. Everything that happens in the world, to the most minute happening, can happen only because God positively wills it. This extends to human lives and thus governs our being, what happens to us, what we do.[8] God's sovereign will has enormous bearing on spirituality, especially through his teachings on calling and purpose. Each person has a vocation, a God-given task in the world, so that generally speaking one is where one should be and doing what one should be doing. Social location and work, in turn, inform one's sense of identity and inspire the meaningfulness of one's work. However, the reality of relative social mobility offered by the printing press and other major economic innovations and the powerful ecclesial changes transpiring in Calvin's Geneva also reflect the way that his notion avoids determinism, inspires creativity, encourages discovery, and centers on improvement. The theme of God's will suffuses Calvin's thinking.

Church as Holy Community. Calvin was much more concerned than Luther that the church be a holy community. The idea of sanctification appears in Luther's later writing on the church; he speaks of the effects of the Spirit sanctifying the community. But in Calvin this theme takes on greater importance. It fits neatly into his ecclesiology where the organizational structure of the church includes an institutional oversight of public behavior. The church as a community mediates the work of God as Word and Spirit. The church functions as the worldly instrument of God's saving activity. Calvin desired that the whole church actually become holy and in so doing leaven and even transform society. Calvin's spirituality is thoroughly ecclesial.

Church and Society. Beginning with the Gregorian Reform in the eleventh century and in its aftermath, the issue of temporal and spiritual power continually flared up. The balance of power between civil rulers, such as kings and princes, and church authorities, such as bishops and their auxiliaries, whose powers were often temporal as well as spiritual, took on local significance in a free city-state such as Geneva. Apart from large political decisions about which among its neighbors Geneva should align with, two groups endowed with authority, the city magistrates and the church ministers were both concerned about public behavior. Calvin taught that church and civil government were two distinct sources of authority, and he provided ways in which they should work in tandem with and support each other. But he also wished to guard the autonomy of church authority, which government was charged to guarantee. The distinctive element of Calvin here, especially relative to Luther, flows precisely from the hand-in-glove relationship of these two distinct sources of spiritual and temporal authority. This vision of cooperation with uniqueness enabled Calvin to articulate a middle way, as opposed to the Anabaptist rejection of civil authority or the Lutheran and Zwinglian imagination of one authority with differing roles. Calvin's formulas for how these two dimensions of human activity relate to each other, to God's will, and to both society and the individual remain classic and not irrelevant, *mutatis mutandis*, to present-day modern democratic societies, especially given their inability to function in a society with either an established or disestablished relationship between ecclesial and civil authorities.

These aspects of Calvin's context and thought help to situate his authorship. They are far from exhaustive, and they are mixed up with one another. Their inner dynamics should come alive in his texts from the *Institutes*. The next step in this Introduction will be to provide a schematic outline of the selected passages.

Calvin on Law, Sanctification, and Vocation

Before we turn to Calvin's short treatise on the Christian life, three short considerations in the *Institutes* will help narrow down the large context to a more focused discussion. These concern ideas that help bring Calvin's distinct spirituality into sharper focus. They treat, first, the positive role of law in the spiritual life, the dynamics of gradual sanctification, and his ideas on vocation or particular station in life.

Law. A sensibility for the value of law, which one would expect of Calvin the lawyer, forms part of his estimation of God's sovereign power and will. In contrast to Luther, Calvin had a stronger and more positive view of the law than his precursor's. The law expresses God's sovereign will. Sensitivity to law, in turn, entails more emphasis on a constructive role that ethics plays in Christian spirituality. Troeltsch observed that the ultimate differences between Luther and Calvin lie not in the area of doctrine but in ethics and its place in the Christian life.[9] Calvin's view of the law includes the two functions it has in Luther: First, the law shows God's righteousness and thus "warns, informs, convicts, and lastly condemns every man of his own unrighteousness"[10] (2.7.6). The negative movement has a positive aspect: Despair moves us to seek grace (2.7.8–9). Second, the law serves to inculcate fear and to restrain sin, as in a kind of forced righteousness.

It acts as a deterrent but has no salvific value. It is "necessary for the public community of men" (2.7.10). On this level the law works outwardly, regulating behavior without supplying internal motivation.

But unlike Luther, Calvin speaks of a third function of the law, one that operates more positively and corresponds to the proper purpose of law: It provides a teaching device for believers and guides them to live according to God's will. The two escorts of human existence are law and the Spirit; the law instructs in the ways of the Spirit (2.7.12). Calvin insists that "the law points out the goal toward which throughout life we are to strive" (2.7.13). "Therefore through Christ the teaching of the law remains inviolable; by teaching, admonishing, reproving, and correcting, it forms us and prepares us for every good work" (2.7.14).

Sanctification. Calvin treats repentance and sanctification as part of the logic of conversion to God. Faith and repentance are two distinct responses to the word of God, but they are inseparable. *Repentance* is defined as turning our life to God. It arises from true or holy awe-filled fear of God; it includes mortification or denial of the flesh or the "old man," and in a vivification or life in the Spirit; it can be called a new life in Christ. It is a turning around, a conversion, a "departing from ourselves, [whereby] we turn to God, and having taken off our former mind, we put on a new" [one] (3.3.5). Repentance involves a spiritual reorientation of the self with respect to God (3.3.6), a rebirth and participation in Christ; one is regenerated, born again into the righteousness of Jesus Christ by adhering to him. This is not far from Luther. But in Calvin regeneration does not happen all at once; persons grow in their closeness to Christ toward a gradual restoration of the image of God (3.3.9). This element of growth in sanctification is a major characteristic of Calvin's treatise on the spiritual life. The believer remains both a sinner and justified: Believers are still sinners. Concupiscence remains because one cannot escape one's flesh and its tendency to sin. But in Calvin's view, while believers are still sinners, sin has lost its dominion in their lives, and they grow closer to God.

Vocation. Calvin did not live in a time of fluid social mobility; social standing then would be considered fixed by today's standards. However, new opportunities wrought by the seismic shifts of the printing press and the ecclesial upheaval in the generation preceding Calvin suited a notion of vocation that encouraged contentment in one's location and circumstances but with spiritual agency and practical theology for improvement and transformation. Within this given cultural standard Calvin assigns a positive dimension to each role in life and to the particular performance of the person in it. Given God's sovereignty and all-encompassing will, and given the positive value of law and growth through the positive performance of one's duties, Calvin can say that God "has appointed duties for every man in his particular way of life" (3.10.6). Calvin says this to warn people against resenting their stations in life. But the caution has a positive side: Everyone's actual situation provides a framework for an integrated life that corresponds to the will of God. Calvin thinks that every person's actual calling in life specifies the vehicle of that person's sanctification. Relative to each particular calling in life, he says: "From this will arise also a singular consolation: that no task will be so sordid and base, provided you obey your calling in it, that it will not shine and be reckoned very precious in God's sight" (3.10.6).

Calvin on the Christian Life

Calvin's short treatise on the Christian life is a section of his *Institutes of the Christian Religion.* The first edition of 1536 steadily grew until the final Latin and French versions of 1559 and 1560. These editions contain four books that roughly concern God, Christ, the way we receive the grace of Christ, and, finally, the church; the work ends with a brief instruction on the relation between church and state.

The treatise on the Christian life, which was originally one chapter, was later divided into five chapters of Book III on the reception of the salvation mediated by Christ. This occurs through faith, which entails justification, regeneration, and sanctification. Importantly, Calvin reverses the order and treats sanctification first. The treatise on the Christian life expands in a more specific language the discussion of regeneration and sanctification that are entailed in faith. Calvin develops further how conversion plays itself out in the Christian life. Ideally, the Christian life is growth in sanctification. One can imagine two aspects to the Christian life, one negative and the other positive. The negative is self-denial; the positive is turning to Christ and participating in Christ's life. For Calvin, Christian spirituality is Christian life in the Christian society of Geneva.[11]

The treatise in its final development has five parts, the five chapters (6–10) of Book III. Calvin begins with an appeal to scripture on the subject. He then moves to the negative side of Christian life: a chapter on denial of self and self-discipline and another on bearing the cross. He then treats meditation on the future life with Christ (eschatology) and how to live in the present. The result is a neat self-contained treatise on Calvin's spirituality narrowly conceived. A schematic outline of the contents of each chapter will set up a closer reading of the text.

Scripture on the Christian Life (3.6). In the first chapter of five, Calvin turns to scripture for the basic attitudes or motives of the Christian life. God is holy and righteous; God has no fellowship with impurity and unrighteousness. A basic desire to become more acceptable to God motivates Christian spirituality; even though this is not in our own power, the Christian responds to the summons of the Spirit as guided by the law (3.6.2).

Christ in particular drives a Christian life. Christians conform themselves to him as the primary image of God. This follows the logic of the imitation of Christ; Christians strive to make themselves into Christ's image (3.6.3).

Calvin, however, warns that, in the end, knowledge of Christ is not a question of words but one of action (3.3.4). No one can become perfect in this world, but all should do all that is within their capacity. We remain imperfect, but the effort of striving counts (3.3.5).

The Sum of Christian Life Is Denial of Self (3.7). The second chapter on the Christian life lays down three more axioms for self-understanding before God. The first reminds Christians that they belong to God, so they should offer themselves to God as a proper sacrifice. The ideal points to transcending the self, forgetting the self, and all that is ours, and, conversely, living for God (3.7.1). These radical sayings recall the monastic tradition; they raise up the virtue of submission—that is, obedience to God.

The second principle marks the other side of the first: The Christian should live not for the self but for God's will and for everything that advances God's glory (3.7.2). Things of the flesh, worldly lusts, are condemned; reason, mind over matter, equity, sobriety, balance, industry are all recommended as virtues in service of God and God's glory (3.7.3). This evangelical language seems to distance Calvin from an ethics of self-fulfillment or the achievement of happiness, which provides a framework for the virtue ethics of Thomas Aquinas.

The third principle has to do with love of neighbor and social life. Self-denial finds its primary rationale in relation to God, but it relates also to other people (3.7.4). Calvin recommends subordination of our own benefit for the good of others. He also stresses the community and the building up of the ecclesial body of Christ as a value (3.7.5). Others are loved not for their own sake, of course, but for God's sake and God's image within them that is worthy of love (3.7.6). Self-denial in the Christian life is principally directed to God;

those who act according to their own plan and not God's live restlessly and uneasily (3.7.8).

Bearing the Cross (3.8). The third chapter on the Christian life presents a theology of bearing the cross. The cross symbolizes the hardships of life. Bearing the cross establishes a fellowship with Christ. Following Christ entails willingness to bear suffering for and with Christ as a sign of fellowship (3.8.1). The cross leads to trust in God's power rather than in one's own. In trust, Christians acknowledge their own incapacity, and their doing so leads to humility and looking to God (3.8.2). The cross serves as medicine and self-discipline and can be looked upon as God's fatherly correction (3.8.5–6).

Meditation on the Future Life (3.9). Fourth, Calvin sets the Christian life in an eschatological framework: The Christian should live within the horizon of the end time. In the face of adversity, "[W]e must ever look to this end: to accustom ourselves to contempt for the present life and to be aroused thereby to meditate on the future life" (3.9.1). Even though life may be filled with pain, the Christian should still look upon the world as a blessing of God. Even the sufferings in this world can be seen as a blessing because they urge people to long for eternal life. In every case, then, Christians should have gratitude to God for earthly existence as they prepare for the kingdom of God by their lives in this world (3.9.3). Calvin's thought here has spiritual substance beneath the somewhat moralistic presentation. Calvin's emphasis on the coming kingdom drives and motivates effort and forbearance. It orients the human effort and aligns all earthly activity with the great image of the perfect will of God that will reign in the coming Kingship of Jesus. It is the spirituality that nourishes a life of fallible human effort and guarantees the fulfillment of Christian sanctification, which involves the righteousness of all of life.

How to Make Use of the Present Life and Its Supports (3.10). This fifth section of the treatise has a slightly different tone from that of the others: Calvin seems to reinforce traditional pious language with practical humanist principles that deal with the concrete world. What maxims support life in the world today? The good things of this world are to be used and enjoyed as gifts of God while maintaining an inner balance between self-denial and delight. We are pilgrims, and we need rules of life for the journey that fall between strictness and laxity, not a purely negative norm of being against pleasure and not a tolerance of indulgence. Scripture provides such norms (3.10.1).

The main principle for Calvin is this: Things should be used according to the end destined by God, who created them (3.10.2).[12] This end also includes our enjoyment and pleasure—for example, delight in material beauty (3.10.2). Creatures should be enjoyed, if that is what they are for; mere necessity should not be the norm, for it would treat human beings like blocks of stone. Yet immoderation should be avoided, as in lust and so on. Calvin seems to embrace the Aristotelian mean between extreme responses as the ideal. "We are not to seek these blessings indulgently, or to seek wealth greedily, but to serve dutifully in our calling."[13]

From the contemplation of eternity, Calvin derives three rules for the use of creatures: First, use creatures, but use them as if one did not use them in themselves; that is, do not invest intrinsic value to creatures because they are means rather than ends. The second rule is patience in one's poverty, because frugality in one's lifestyle is a virtue (3.10.5). It was noted earlier that, because each person has a calling and vocation in life, Calvin did not expect social mobility. Particular providence means that each one has his or her own particular calling—that is, a God-assigned place in life. Patience within that sphere thus corresponds to a natural social virtue. The third rule is called the principle of stewardship. It regulates the use of earthly goods. It "decrees that all those things were so given to us by the kindness of God, and so destined for our benefit, that they are, as it were, entrusted to us, and we must one day render account of them" (3.10.5). Few of Calvin's principles are as relevant today as this one. But note that it is a religious principle and not as pragmatic as it appears in a secular culture.

These texts provide a framework for appreciating the pointed evangelical synthesis that was uniquely Calvin's as he fashioned a new interpretation of Christian spirituality for his time and his particular location, even as he inspired a movement of reform with the intent of a wider-ranging renewal. Like all classics, this synthesis became relevant for Christians across the continent and remains important today.

Notes

1. Alister E. McGrath, *A Life of John Calvin: A Study in the Shaping of Western Culture* (Oxford: Basil Blackwell, 1990), xii.

2. Ibid.

3. Ibid., 60.

4. John Calvin, *Institutes of the Christian Religion (1536)*, ed. H. H. Meeter Center for Calvin Studies (Grand Rapids, MI: Eerdmans, 1986).

5. Ernst Troeltsch, *The Social Teaching of the Christian Churches* (New York: Harper Torchbooks, 1960), 576–617, draws these lines very distinctly.

6. E. William Monter, in *Calvin's Geneva* (Huntington, NY: Robert E. Krieger, 1975), describes the transition. Monter estimated the population of Geneva in 1537 at 10,300. For more in-depth analysis, see Jeffrey R. Watt, *The Consistory and Social Discipline in Calvin's Geneva* (Rochester, NY: University of Rochester Press, 2020).

7. Calvin took his first organizational steps during his first stay in Geneva, but his organizing skills are far more developed in "Draft Ecclesiastical Ordinances (September and October, 1541)," found in *Calvin: Theological Treatises* (London: SCM Press, 1954), 58–72.

8. Much more can and should be said beyond reporting Calvin's teaching in such a stark and blunt fashion. He found this doctrine in Augustine and in certain scriptural texts. There are mitigating

factors to this harsh doctrine, but the subject requires more than is fitting for this short introduction to Calvin's spiritual thought. Many believers consulted the signs of election and found the teaching consoling.

    9. Troeltsch, *Social Teachings*, 624.

    10. John Calvin, *Calvin: Institutes of the Christian Religion*, ed. John T. McNeill (Philadelphia: Westminster Press, 1960), Book 2, Chapter 7, Paragraph 6 (cited in the text as 2.7.6).

    11. It should be stipulated at the outset that Calvin did not separate Christian spirituality from Christian assembly and worship. This consideration of the entwinement of theology, ethics, and spirituality short-circuits a larger discussion of ecclesial life.

    12. This use of creatures sounds like a principle from Ignatius Loyola and his Spiritual Exercises. Did they both learn this at the University of Paris from the noted scholastic ethicist John Major, who taught at Montaigu from 1525 to 1531?

    13. This title in the text was not written by Calvin, but it announces and summarizes paragraphs 3–6 of the chapter.

II

The Texts

John Calvin on the Law: Selections from *Institutes of the Christian Religion*

Book II, Chapter VII, Parts 8–15

8. The punitive function of the law in its work upon believers and unbelievers

The wickedness and condemnation of us all are sealed by the testimony of the law. Yet this is not done to cause us to fall down in despair or, completely discouraged, to rush headlong over the brink—provided we duly profit by the testimony of the law. It is true that in this way the wicked are terrified, but because of their obstinacy of heart. For the children of God the knowledge of the law should have another purpose. The apostle testifies that we are indeed condemned by the judgment of the law, "so that every mouth may be stopped, and the whole world may be held accountable to God" [Rom. 3:19]. He teaches the same idea in yet another place: "For God has shut up all men in unbelief," not that he may destroy all or suffer all to perish, but "that he may have mercy upon all" [Rom. 11:32]. This means that, dismissing the stupid opinion of their own strength, they come to realize that they stand and are upheld by God's hand alone; that, naked and empty-handed, they flee to his mercy, repose entirely in it, hide deep within it, and seize upon it alone for righteousness and merit. For God's mercy is revealed in Christ to all who seek and wait upon it with true faith. In the precepts of the law, God is but the rewarder of perfect righteousness, which all of us lack, and conversely, the severe judge of evil deeds. But in Christ his face shines, full of grace and gentleness, even upon us poor and unworthy sinners.

9. The law, as Augustine states, by accusing moves us to seek grace

Augustine often speaks of the value of calling upon the grace of His help. For example, he writes to Hilary: "The law bids us, as we try to fulfill its requirements, and become wearied in our weakness under it, to know how to ask the help of grace." He writes similarly to Asellius: "The usefulness of the law lies in convicting man of his infirmity and moving him to call upon the remedy of grace which is in Christ." Again, to Innocent of Rome: "The law commands; grace supplies the strength to act." Again, to Valentinus: "God commands what we cannot do that we may know what we ought to seek from him." Again: "The law was given to accuse you; that accused you might fear; that fearing you might beg forgiveness; and that you might not presume on your own strength." Again: "The law was given for this purpose: to make you, being great, little; to show that you do not have in yourself the strength to attain righteousness, and for you, thus helpless, unworthy, and destitute, to flee to grace." Afterward he addresses God: "So act, O Lord; so act, O merciful Lord. Command what cannot be fulfilled. Rather, command what can be fulfilled only through thy grace so that, since men are unable to fulfill it through their own strength, every mouth may be stopped, and no one may seem great to himself. Let all be little ones, and let all the world be guilty before God."

But it is silly of me to amass so many testimonies, since that holy man has written a work specifically on this topic, entitled *On the Spirit and the Letter*. He does not as expressly describe the second value of the law, either because he knew that it depended upon the first, or because he did not grasp it thoroughly, or because he lacked words to express its correct meaning distinctly and plainly enough.

Yet this first function of the law is exercised also in the reprobate. For, although they do not proceed so far with the children of God as to be renewed and bloom again in the inner man after the abasement of their flesh, but are struck dumb by the first terror and lie in despair, nevertheless, the fact that their consciences are buffeted by such waves serves to show forth the equity of the divine judgment. For the reprobate always freely desire to evade God's judgment. Now, although that judgment is not yet revealed, so routed are they by the testimony of the law and of conscience that they betray in themselves what they have deserved.

10. The law as protection of the community from unjust men

The second function of the law is this: at least by fear of punishment to restrain certain men who are untouched by any care for what is just and right unless compelled by hearing the dire threats in the law. But they are restrained, not because their inner mind is stirred or affected, but because, being bridled, so to speak, they keep their hands from outward activity and hold inside the depravity that otherwise they would wantonly have indulged. Consequently, they are neither better nor more righteous before God. Hindered by fright or shame, they dare neither execute what they have conceived in their minds nor openly breathe forth the rage of their lust. Still, they do not have hearts disposed to fear and obedience toward God. Indeed, the more they restrain themselves, the more strongly are they inflamed; they burn and boil within and are ready to do anything or burst forth anywhere—but for the fact that this dread of the law hinders them. Not only that—but so wickedly do they also hate the law itself, and curse God the Lawgiver, that if they could, they would most certainly abolish Him, for they cannot bear him either when he commands them to do right, or when he takes vengeance on the despisers of his majesty. All who are still unregenerate feel—some more obscurely, some more openly—that they are not drawn to obey the law voluntarily but impelled by a violent fear do so against their will and despite their opposition to it.

But this constrained and forced righteousness is necessary for the public community of men, for whose tranquillity the Lord herein provided when he took care that everything be not tumultuously confounded. This would happen if everything were permitted to all men. Nay, even for the children of God, before they are called and while they are destitute of the Spirit of sanctification [Rom. 1:4, Vg. etc.], so long as they play the wanton in the folly of the flesh, it is profitable for them to undergo this tutelage. While by the dread of divine vengeance they are restrained at least from outward wantonness, with minds yet untamed they progress but slightly for the present, yet become partially broken in by bearing the yoke of righteousness. As a consequence, when they are called, they are not utterly untutored and uninitiated in discipline as if it were something unknown. The apostle seems specially to have alluded to this function of the law when he teaches "that the law is not laid down for the just but for the unjust and disobedient, for the ungodly and sinners, for the unholy and profane, for murderers of parents, for manslayers, fornicators, perverts, kidnapers, liars, perjurers, and whatever else runs counter to sound doctrine" [I Tim. 1: 9–10]. He shows in this that the law is like a halter to check the raging and otherwise limitlessly ranging lusts of the flesh.

11. The law a deterrent to those not yet regenerate

What Paul says elsewhere, that "the law was for the Jews a tutor unto Christ" [Gal. 3:24], may be applied to both functions of the law. There are two kinds of men whom the law leads by its tutelage to Christ.

Of the first kind we have already spoken: because they are too full of their own virtue or of the assurance of their own righteousness, they are not fit to receive Christ's grace unless they first be emptied. Therefore, through the recognition of their own misery, the law brings them down to humility in order thus to prepare them to seek what previously they did not realize they lacked.

Men of the second kind have need of a bridle to restrain them from so slackening the reins on the lust of the flesh as to fall clean away from all pursuit of righteousness. For where the Spirit of God does not yet rule, lusts sometimes so boil that there is danger lest they plunge the soul bound over to them into forgetfulness and contempt of God. And such would happen if God did not oppose it with this remedy. Therefore, if he does not immediately regenerate those whom he has destined to inherit his Kingdom, until the time of his visitation, he keeps them safe through the works of the law under fear [cf. I Peter 2:12]. This is not that chaste and pure fear such as ought to be in his sons, but a fear useful in teaching them true godliness according to their capacity. We have so many proofs of this matter that no example is needed. For all who have at any time groped about in ignorance of God will admit that it happened to them in such a way that the bridle of the law restrained them in some fear and reverence toward God until, regenerated by the Spirit, they began wholeheartedly to love him.

12. Even the believers have need of the law

The third and principal use, which pertains more closely to the proper purpose of the law, finds its place among believers in whose hearts the Spirit of God already lives and reigns. For even though they have the law written and engraved upon their hearts by the finger of God [Jer. 31:33; Heb. 10:16], that is, have been so moved and quickened through the directing of the Spirit that they long to obey God, they still profit by the law in two ways.

Here is the best instrument for them to learn more thoroughly each day the nature of the Lord's will to which they aspire, and to confirm them in the understanding of it. It is as if some servant, already prepared with all earnestness of heart to commend himself to his master, must search out and observe his master's ways more carefully in order to conform and accommodate himself to them. And not one of us may escape from this necessity. For no man has heretofore attained to such wisdom as to be unable, from the daily instruction of the law, to make fresh progress toward a purer knowledge of the divine will.

Again, because we need not only teaching but also exhortation, the servant of God will also avail himself of this benefit of the law: by frequent meditation upon it to be aroused to obedience, be strengthened in it, and be drawn back from the slippery path of transgression. In this way the saints must press on, for, however eagerly they may in accordance with the Spirit strive toward God's righteousness, the listless flesh always so burdens them that they do not proceed with due readiness. The law is to the flesh like a whip to an idle and balky ass, to arouse it to work. Even for a spiritual man not yet free of the weight of the flesh the law remains a constant sting that will not let him stand still. Doubtless David was referring to this use when he sang the praises of the law: "The law of the Lord is spotless, converting souls; . . . the righteous acts of the Lord are right, rejoicing hearts; the precept of the

Lord is clear, enlightening the eyes," etc. [Ps. 18: 8–9, Vg.; 19:7–8, EV]. Likewise: "Thy word is a lamp to my feet and a light to my path" [Ps. 119:105], and innumerable other sayings in the same psalm [e.g., Ps. 119:5]. These do not contradict Paul's statements, which show not what use the law serves for the regenerate, but what it can of itself confer upon man. But here the prophet proclaims the great usefulness of the law: the Lord instructs by their reading of it those whom he inwardly instills with a readiness to obey. He lays hold not only of the precepts, but the accompanying promise of grace, which alone sweetens what is bitter. For what would be less lovable than the law if, with importuning and threatening alone, it troubled souls through fear, and distressed them through fright? David especially shows that in the law he apprehended the Mediator, without whom there is no delight or sweetness.

13. Whoever wants to do away with the law entirely for the faithful, understands it falsely

Certain ignorant persons, not understanding this distinction, rashly cast out the whole of Moses, and bid farewell to the two Tables of the Law. For they think it obviously alien to Christians to hold to a doctrine that contains the "dispensation of death" [cf. II Cor. 3:7]. Banish this wicked thought from our minds! For Moses has admirably taught that the law, which among sinners can engender nothing but death, ought among the saints to have a better and more excellent use. When about to die, he decreed to the people as follows: "Lay to your hearts all the words which this day I enjoin upon you, that you may command them to your children, and teach them to keep, do, and fulfill all those things written in the book of this law. For they have not been commanded to you in vain, but for each to live in them" [Deut. 32: 46–47, cf. Vg.]. But if no one can deny that a perfect pattern of righteousness stands forth in the law, either we need no rule to live rightly and justly, or it is forbidden to depart from the law. There are not many rules, but one everlasting and unchangeable rule to live by. For this reason we are not to refer solely to one age David's statement that the life of a righteous man is a continual meditation upon the law [Ps. 1:2], for it is just as applicable to every age, even to the end of the world.

We ought not to be frightened away from the law or to shun its instruction merely because it requires a much stricter moral purity than we shall reach while we bear about with us the prison house of our body. For the law is not now acting toward us as a rigorous enforcement officer who is not satisfied unless the requirements are met. But in this perfection to which it exhorts us, the law points out the goal toward which throughout life we are to strive. In this the law is no less profitable than consistent with our duty. If we fail not in this struggle, it is well. Indeed, this whole life is a race [cf. I Cor. 9:24–26]; when its course has been run, the Lord will grant us to attain that goal to which our efforts now press forward from afar.

14. To what extent has the law been abrogated for believers?

Now, the law has power to exhort believers. This is not a power to bind their consciences with a curse, but one to shake off their sluggishness, by repeatedly urging them, and to pinch them awake to their imperfection. Therefore, many persons, wishing to express such liberation from that curse, say that for believers the law—I am still speaking of the moral law— has been abrogated. Not that the law no longer enjoins believers to do what is right, but only that it is not for them what it formerly was: it may no longer condemn and destroy their consciences by frightening and confounding them.

Paul teaches clearly enough such an abrogation of the law
[cf. Rom. 7:6]. That the Lord also preached it appears from
this: he would not have refuted the notion that he would
abolish the law [Matt. 5:17] if this opinion had not been
prevalent among the Jews. But since without some pretext
the idea could not have arisen by chance, it may be supposed
to have arisen from a false interpretation of his teaching, just
as almost all errors have commonly taken their occasion from
truth. But to avoid stumbling on the same stone, let us accu-
rately distinguish what in the law has been abrogated from
what still remains in force. When the Lord testifies that he
"came not to abolish the law but to fulfill it" and that "until
heaven and earth pass away . . . not a jot will pass away from
the law until all is accomplished" [Matt. 5:17–18], he sufficiently confirms that by his coming nothing is going to be
taken away from the observance of the law. And justly—inasmuch as he came rather to remedy transgressions of it.
Therefore through Christ the teaching of the law remains
inviolable; by teaching, admonishing, reproving, and correcting, it forms us and prepares us for every good work [cf. II
Tim. 3:16–17].

15. The law is abrogated to the extent that it no longer condemns us

What Paul says of the curse unquestionably applies not to
the ordinance itself but solely to its force to bind the conscience. The law not only teaches but forthrightly enforces
what it commands. If it be not obeyed—indeed, if one in any
respect fails in his duty—the law unleashes the thunderbolt
of its curse. For this reason the apostle says: "All who are of
the works of the law are under a curse; for it is written, 'Cursed
be every one who does not fulfill all things'" [Gal. 3:10; Deut.
27:26 p.]. He describes as "under the works of the law" those

who do not ground their righteousness in remission of sins, through which we are released from the rigor of the law. He therefore teaches that we must be released from the bonds of the law, unless we wish to perish miserably under them.

But from what bonds? The bonds of harsh and dangerous requirements, which remit nothing of the extreme penalty of the law, and suffer no transgression to go unpunished. To redeem us from this curse, I say, Christ was made a curse for us. "For it is written: 'Cursed be every one who hangs on a tree'" [Gal. 3:13; Deut. 21:23]. In the following chapter Paul teaches that Christ was made subject to the law [Gal. 4:4] "that he might redeem those under the law" [Gal. 4:5a, Vg.]. This means the same thing, for he continues: "So that we might receive by adoption the right of sons" [Gal. 4:5b]. What does this mean? That we should not be borne down by an unending bondage, which would agonize our consciences with the fear of death. Meanwhile this always remains an unassailable fact: no part of the authority of the law is withdrawn without our having always to receive it with the same veneration and obedience.

John Calvin on Sanctification: Selections from *Institutes of the Christian Religion*

Book III, Chapter III, Parts 4–10

4. Penance under law and under gospel

Others, because they saw the various meanings of this word in Scripture, posited two forms of repentance. To distinguish them by some mark, they called one "repentance of the law." Through it the sinner, wounded by the branding of sin and stricken by dread of God's wrath, remains caught in that disturbed state and cannot extricate himself from it. The other they call "repentance of the gospel." Through it the sinner is indeed sorely afflicted, but rises above it and lays hold of Christ as medicine for his wound, comfort for his dread, the haven of his misery. They offer as examples of "repentance of the law" Cain [Gen. 4:13], Saul [I Sam. 15:30], and Judas [Matt. 27:4]. While Scripture recounts their repentance to us, it represents them as acknowledging the gravity of their sin, and afraid of God's wrath; but since they conceived of God only as Avenger and Judge, that very thought overwhelmed them. Therefore their repentance was nothing but a sort of entryway of hell, which they had already entered in this life, and had begun to undergo punishment before the wrath of

God's majesty. We see "gospel repentance" in all those who, made sore by the sting of sin but aroused and refreshed by trust in God's mercy, have turned to the Lord. When Hezekiah received the message of death, he was stricken with fear. But he wept and prayed and, looking to God's goodness, he recovered confidence [II Kings 20:2; Isa. 38:2]. The Ninevites were troubled by a horrible threat of destruction; but putting on sackcloth and ashes, they prayed, hoping that the Lord might be turned toward them and be turned away from the fury of his wrath [Jonah 3:5, 9]. David confessed that he sinned greatly in taking a census of the people, but he added, "O Lord, . . . take away the iniquity of thy servant" [II Sam. 24:10]. When he was rebuked by Nathan, David acknowledged his sin of adultery, and he fell down before the Lord, but at the same time he awaited pardon [II Sam. 12:13, 16]. Such was the repentance of those who felt remorse of heart at Peter's preaching; but, trusting in God's goodness, they added: "Brethren, what shall we do?" [Acts 2:37]. Such, also, was Peter's own repentance; he wept bitterly indeed [Matt. 26:75; Luke 22:62], but he did not cease to hope.

5. Definition

Although all these things are true, yet the word "repentance" itself, so far as I can learn from Scripture, is to be understood otherwise. For their inclusion of faith under repentance disagrees with what Paul says in Acts: "Testifying both to Jews and Gentiles of repentance to God, and of faith . . . in Jesus Christ" [Acts 20:21]. There he reckons repentance and faith as two different things. What then? Can true repentance stand, apart from faith? Not at all. But even though they cannot be separated, they ought to be distinguished. As faith is not without hope, yet faith and hope are different things, so repentance and faith, although they are held together by a permanent bond, require to be joined rather than confused.

Indeed, I am aware of the fact that the whole of conversion to God is understood under the term "repentance," and faith is not the least part of conversion; but in what sense this is so will very readily appear when its force and nature are explained. The Hebrew word for "repentance" is derived from conversion or return; the Greek word, from change of mind or of intention. And the thing itself corresponds closely to the etymology of both words. The meaning is that, departing from ourselves, we turn to God, and having taken off our former mind, we put on a new. On this account, in my judgment, repentance can thus be well defined: it is the true turning of our life to God, a turning that arises from a pure and earnest fear of him; and it consists in the mortification of our flesh and of the old man, and in the vivification of the Spirit.

In that sense we must understand all those preachings by which either the prophets of old or the apostles later exhorted men of their time to repentance. For they were striving for this one thing: that, confused by their sins and pierced by the fear of divine judgment, they should fall down and humble themselves before him whom they had offended, and with true repentance return into the right path. Therefore these words are used interchangeably in the same sense: "Turn or return to the Lord," "repent," and "do penance" [Matt. 3:2]. Whence even the Sacred History says that "penance is done after God," where men who had lived wantonly in their own lusts, neglecting him, begin to obey his Word [I Sam. 7:2–3] and are ready to go where their leader calls them. And John and Paul use the expression "Producing fruits worthy of repentance" [Luke 3:8; Acts 26:20; cf. Rom. 6:4] for leading a life that demonstrates and testifies in all its actions repentance of this sort.

6. Repentance as turning to God

But before we go further, it will be useful to explain more clearly the definition that we have laid down. We must examine repentance mainly under three heads. First, when we call it a "turning of life to God," we require a transformation, not only in outward works, but in the soul itself. Only when it puts off its old nature does it bring forth the fruits of works in harmony with its renewal. The prophet, wishing to express this change, bids whom he calls to repentance to get themselves a new heart [Ezek. 18:31]. Moses, therefore, intending to show how the Israelites might repent and be duly turned to the Lord, often teaches that it be done with "all the heart" and "all the soul" [Deut. 6:5; 10:12; 30:2, 6, 10]. This expression we see frequently repeated by the prophets [Jer. 24:7]. Moses also, in calling it "circumcision of heart," searches the inmost emotions [Deut. 10:16; 30:6]. No passage, however, better reveals the true character of repentance than Jer., ch. 4: "If you return, O Israel," says the Lord, "return to me. . . . Plow up your arable land and do not sow among thorns. Circumcise yourselves to the Lord, and remove the foreskin of your hearts" [vs. 1, 3–4]. See how he declares that they will achieve nothing in taking up the pursuit of righteousness unless wickedness be first of all cast out from their inmost heart. And to move them thoroughly he warns them that it is with God that they have to deal, with whom shifts avail nothing, for He hates a double heart [cf. James 1:8]. Isaiah for this reason satirizes the gauche efforts of hypocrites who were actively striving after outward repentance in ceremonies while they made no effort to undo the burden of injustice with which they bound the poor [Isa. 58:6]. There he also beautifully shows in what duties unfeigned repentance properly consists.

7. Repentance as induced by the fear of God?

The second point was our statement that repentance proceeds from an earnest fear of God. For, before the mind of the sinner inclines to repentance, it must be aroused by thinking upon divine judgment. When this thought is deeply and thoroughly fixed in mind—that God will someday mount his judgment seat to demand a reckoning of all words and deeds—it will not permit the miserable man to rest nor to breathe freely even for a moment without stirring him continually to reflect upon another mode of life whereby he may be able to stand firm in that judgment. For this reason, Scripture often mentions judgment when it urges to repentance, as in the prophecy of Jeremiah: "Lest perchance my wrath go forth like fire . . . , and there be no one to quench it, because of the evil of your doings" [Jer. 4:4 p.]. In Paul's sermon to the Athenians: "Although God has hitherto overlooked the times of this ignorance, he now calls upon all men everywhere to repent because he has fixed a day on which he will judge the world in equity" [Acts 17:30–31, cf. Vg.]. And in many other passages.

Sometimes by punishments already inflicted Scripture declares God to be judge in order that sinners may reflect on the greater punishments that threaten if they do not repent in time. You have an example of this in Deut., ch. 29 [vs. 19 ff.]. Inasmuch as conversion begins with dread and hatred of sin, the apostle makes "the sorrow . . . according to God" the cause of repentance [II Cor. 7:10, cf. Vg.]. He calls it "sorrow . . . according to God" when we not only abhor punishment but hate and abominate sin itself, because we know that it displeases God. And no wonder! For if we were not sharply pricked, the slothfulness of our flesh could not be corrected. Indeed, these prickings would not have sufficed against its dullness and blockishness had God not penetrated more deeply in unsheathing his rods. There is, besides, an obstinacy that must be beaten down as if with hammers. Therefore, the depravity of our nature compels God to use severity in threatening us. For it would be vain for him gently to allure those who are asleep. I do not list the texts that we repeatedly come upon. There is also another reason why fear of God is the beginning of repentance. For even though the life of man be replete with all the virtues, if it is not directed to the worship of God, it can indeed be praised by the world; but in heaven it will be sheer abomination, since the chief part of righteousness is to render to God his right and honor, of which he is impiously defrauded when we do not intend to subject ourselves to his control.

8. Mortification and vivification as component parts of repentance

In the third place it remains for us to explain our statement that repentance consists of two parts: namely, mortification of the flesh and vivification of the spirit. The prophets express it clearly—although simply and rudely, in accordance with the capacity of the carnal folk—when they say: "Cease to do evil, and do good" [Ps. 36:8, 3, 27, conflated, Vg.]. Likewise, "Wash yourselves; make yourselves clean; remove the evil of your doings from before my eyes; cease to do evil; learn to do good; seek judgment; help the oppressed" [Isa. 1:16–17, cf. Vg., etc.]. For when they recall man from evil, they demand the destruction of the whole flesh, which is full of evil and of perversity. It is a very hard and difficult thing to put off ourselves and to depart from our inborn disposition. Nor can we think of the flesh as completely destroyed unless we have wiped out whatever we have from ourselves. But since all emotions of the flesh are hostility against God [cf. Rom. 8:7], the first step toward obeying his law is to deny our own nature. Afterward, they designate the renewal by the fruits that follow from it—namely, righteousness, judgment, and mercy. It would not be enough duly to discharge such duties unless the mind itself and the heart first put on the inclination to righteousness, judgment, and mercy. That comes to pass when the Spirit of God so imbues our souls, steeped in his holiness, with both new thoughts and feelings, that they can be rightly considered new. Surely, as we are naturally turned away from God, unless self-denial precedes, we shall never approach that which is right. Therefore, we are very often enjoined to put off the old man, to renounce the world and the flesh, to bid our evil desires farewell, to be renewed in the spirit of our mind [Eph. 4:22–23]. Indeed, the very word "mortification" warns us how difficult it is to forget our previous nature. For from "mortification" we infer that we are not conformed to the fear of God and do not learn the rudiments of piety, unless we are violently slain by the sword of the Spirit and brought to nought. As if God had declared that for us to be reckoned among his children our common nature must die!

9. Rebirth in Christ!

Both things happen to us by participation in Christ. For if we truly partake in his death, "our old man is crucified by his power, and the body of sin perishes" [Rom. 6:6 p.], that the corruption of original nature may no longer thrive. If we share in his resurrection, through it we are raised up into newness of life to correspond with the righteousness of God. Therefore, in a word, I interpret repentance as regeneration, whose sole end is to restore in us the image of God that had been disfigured and all but obliterated through Adam's transgression. So the apostle teaches when he says: "Now we, with unveiled face, beholding the glory of the Lord, are being changed into his likeness from glory to glory even as from the Spirit of the Lord" [II Cor. 3:18]. Likewise, another passage: "Be ye renewed in the spirit of your mind, and put on the new man which is after God created in righteousness and holiness of truth" [Eph. 4:23, Vg.]. "Putting on the new man . . . who is being renewed into the knowledge and the image of him who created him" [Col. 3:10, cf. Vg.]. Accordingly, we are restored by this regeneration through the benefit of Christ into the righteousness of God; from which we had fallen through Adam. In this way it pleases the Lord fully to restore whomsoever he adopts into the inheritance of life. And indeed, this restoration does not take place in one moment or one day or one year; but through continual and sometimes even slow advances God wipes out in his elect the corruptions of the flesh, cleanses them of guilt, consecrates them to himself as temples renewing all their minds to true purity that they may practice repentance throughout their lives and know that this warfare will end only at death. All the greater is the depravity of that foul wrangler and apostate Staphylus, who babbles that I confuse the state of present life with heavenly glory when from Paul I interpret the image of God [II Cor. 4:4] as "true holiness and righteousness" [cf. Eph. 4:24]. As if when anything is defined we should not seek its very integrity and perfection. Now this is not to deny a place for growth; rather I say, the closer any man comes to the likeness of God, the more the image of God shines in him. In order that believers may reach this goal, God assigns to them a race of repentance, which they are to run throughout their lives.

10. Believers are still sinners

Thus, then, are the children of God freed through regeneration from bondage to sin. Yet they do not obtain full possession of freedom so as to feel no more annoyance from their flesh, but there still remains in them a continuing occasion for struggle whereby they may be exercised; and not only be exercised, but also better learn their own weakness. In this matter all writers of sounder judgment agree that there remains in a regenerate man a smoldering cinder of evil, from which desires continually leap forth to allure and spur him to commit sin. They also admit that the saints are as yet so bound by that disease of concupiscence that they cannot withstand being at times tickled and incited either to lust or to avarice or to ambition, or to other vices. And we do not need to labor much over investigating what ancient writers thought about this; Augustine alone will suffice for this purpose, since he faithfully and diligently collected the opinions of all. Let my readers, therefore, obtain from him whatever certainty they desire concerning the opinion of antiquity.

But between Augustine and us we can see that there is this difference of opinion: while he concedes that believers, as long as they dwell in mortal bodies, are so bound by inordinate desires that they are unable not to desire inordinately, yet he dare not call this disease "sin." Content to designate it with the term "weakness," he teaches that it becomes sin only when either act or consent follows the conceiving or apprehension of it, that is, when the will yields to the first strong inclination. We, on the other hand, deem it sin when man is tickled by any desire at all against the law of God. Indeed, we label "sin" that very depravity which begets in us desires of this sort. We accordingly teach that in the saints, until they are divested of mortal bodies, there is always sin; for in their flesh there resides that depravity of inordinate desiring which contends against righteousness. And Augustine does not always refrain from using the term "sin," as when he says: "Paul calls by the name 'sin,' the source from which all sins rise up into carnal desire. As far as this pertains to the saints, it loses its dominion on earth and perishes in heaven." By these words he admits that insofar as believers are subject to the inordinate desires of the flesh they are guilty of sin.

John Calvin on the Christian Life: Selections from *Institutes of the Christian Religion*

Book III, Chapters VI–X

CHAPTER VI
THE LIFE OF THE CHRISTIAN MAN; AND FIRST,
BY WHAT ARGUMENTS SCRIPTURE URGES US TO IT

1. Plan of the treatise

The object of regeneration, as we have said, is to manifest in the life of believers a harmony and agreement between God's righteousness and their obedience, and thus to confirm the adoption that they have received as sons [Gal. 4:5; cf. II Peter 1:10].

The law of God contains in itself that newness by which his image can be restored in us. But because our slowness needs many goads and helps, it will be profitable to assemble from various passages of Scripture a pattern for the conduct of life in order that those who heartily repent may not err in their zeal.

Now, in setting forth how the life of a Christian man is to be ordered, I am not unaware that I am entering into a varied and diverse subject, which in magnitude would occupy a large volume, were I to try to treat it in full detail. In composing exhortations on but a single virtue, the ancient doctors, as we see, became very prolix. Yet in this they waste no words. For when a man sets out to commend any one virtue in his discourse, abundance of material drives him to a style of such fullness that he seems not to treat it properly unless he speaks at length. But I do not intend to develop, here, the instruction in living that I am now about to offer to the point of describing individual virtues at length, and of digressing into exhortations. Such may be sought from others' writings, especially from the homilies of the fathers. To show the godly man how he may be directed to a rightly ordered life, and briefly to set down some universal rule with which to determine his duties—this will be quite enough for me. Perhaps there will be opportunity for declamations, or I may turn over to others the tasks for which I am not so well suited. By nature I love brevity; and perhaps if I wished to speak more amply it would not be successful. But though a more extended form of teaching were highly acceptable, I would nevertheless scarcely care to undertake it. Moreover, the plan of the present work demands that we give a simple outline of doctrine as briefly as possible.

As philosophers have fixed limits of the right and the honorable, whence they derive individual duties and the whole company of virtues, so Scripture is not without its own order in this matter, but holds to a most beautiful dispensation, and one much more certain than all the philosophical ones. The only difference is that they, as they were ambitious men, diligently strove to attain an exquisite clarity of order to show the nimbleness of their wit. But the Spirit of God, because he taught without affectation, did not adhere so exactly or continuously to a methodical plan; yet when he lays one down anywhere he hints enough that it is not to be neglected by us.

2. Motives for the Christian life

Now this Scriptural instruction of which we speak has two main aspects. The first is that the love of righteousness, to which we are otherwise not at all inclined by nature, may be instilled and established in our hearts; the second, that a rule be set forth for us that does not let us wander about in our zeal for righteousness.

There are in Scripture very many and excellent reasons for commending righteousness, not a few of which we have already noted in various places. And we shall briefly touch upon still others here. From what foundation may righteousness better arise than from the Scriptural warning that we must be made holy because our God is holy? [Lev. 19:2; I Peter 1:15–16]. Indeed, though we had been dispersed like stray sheep and scattered through the labyrinth of the world, he has gathered us together again to join us with himself. When we hear mention of our union with God, let us remember that holiness must be its bond; not because we come into communion with him by virtue of our holiness! Rather, we ought first to cleave unto him so that, infused with his holiness, we may follow whither he calls. But since it is especially characteristic of his glory that he have no fellowship with wickedness and uncleanness, Scripture accordingly teaches that this is the goal of our calling to which we must ever look if we would answer God when he calls [Isa. 35:8, etc.]. For to what purpose are we rescued from the wickedness and pollution of the world in which we were submerged if we allow ourselves throughout life to wallow in these? Moreover, at the same time Scripture admonishes us that to be reckoned among the people of the Lord we must dwell in the holy city of Jerusalem [cf. Ps. 116:19; 122:2–9]. As he has consecrated this city to himself, it is unlawful to profane it with the impurity of its inhabitants. Whence these declarations: there will be a place in God's Tabernacle for those who walk without blemish and strive after righteousness [Ps. 15:1–2; cf. Ps. 14:1–2, Vg.; cf. also Ps. 24:3–4]. For it is highly unfitting that the sanctuary in which he dwells should like a stable be crammed with filth.

3. The Christian life receives its strongest motive to God's work through the person and redemptive act of Christ

And to wake us more effectively, Scripture shows that God the Father, as he has reconciled us to himself in his Christ [cf. II Cor. 5:18], has in him stamped for us the likeness [cf. Heb. 1:3] to which he would have us conform. Now, let these persons who think that moral philosophy is duly and systematically set forth solely among philosophers find me among the philosophers a more excellent dispensation. They, while they wish particularly to exhort us to virtue, announce merely that we should live in accordance with nature. But Scripture draws its exhortation from the true fountain. It not only enjoins us to refer our life to God, its author, to whom it is bound; but after it has taught that we have degenerated from the true origin and condition of our creation, it also adds that Christ, through whom we return into favor with God, has been set before us as an example, whose pattern we ought to express in our life. What more effective thing can you require than this one thing? Nay, what can you require beyond this one thing? For we have been adopted as sons by the Lord with this one condition: that our life express Christ, the bond of our adoption. Accordingly, unless we give and devote ourselves to righteousness, we not only revolt from our Creator with wicked perfidy, but we also abjure our Savior himself.

Then the Scripture finds occasion for exhortation in all the benefits of God that it lists for us, and in the individual parts of our salvation. Ever since God revealed himself Father to us, we must prove our ungratefulness to him if we did not in turn show ourselves his sons [Mal. 1:6; Eph. 5:1; I John 3:1]. Ever since Christ cleansed us with the washing of his blood, and imparted this cleansing through baptism, it would be unfitting to befoul ourselves with new pollutions [Eph. 5:26; Heb. 10:10; I Cor. 6:11; I Peter 1:15, 19]. Ever since he engrafted us into his body, we must take especial care not to disfigure ourselves, who are his members, with any spot or blemish [Eph. 5:23–33; I Cor. 6:15; John 15:3–6]. Ever since Christ himself, who is our Head, ascended into heaven, it behooves us, having laid aside love of earthly things, wholeheartedly to aspire heavenward [Col. 3:1 ff.]. Ever since the Holy Spirit dedicated us as temples to God, we must take care that God's glory shine through us, and must not commit anything to defile ourselves with the filthiness of sin [I Cor. 3:16; 6:19; II Cor. 6:16]. Ever since both our souls and bodies were destined for heavenly incorruption and an unfading crown [I Peter 5:4], we ought to strive manfully to keep them pure and uncorrupted until the Day of the Lord [I Thess. 5:23; cf. Phil. 1:10]. These, I say, are the most auspicious foundations upon which to establish one's life. One would look in vain for the like of these among the philosophers, who, in their commendation of virtue, never rise above the natural dignity of man.

4. The Christian life is not a matter of the tongue but of the inmost heart

And this is the place to upbraid those who, having nothing but the name and badge of Christ, yet wish to call themselves "Christians." Yet, how shamelessly do they boast of his sacred name? Indeed, there is no intercourse with Christ save for those who have perceived the right understanding of Christ from the word of the gospel. Yet the apostle says that all those who were not taught that they must put on him have not rightly learned Christ, as they have not put off the old man, who is corrupt through deceptive desires [Eph. 4:22, 24]. Therefore, it is proved that they have falsely, and also unjustly, pretended the knowledge of Christ, whatever they meanwhile learnedly and volubly prate about the gospel. For it is a doctrine not of the tongue but of life. It is not apprehended by the understanding and memory alone, as other disciplines are, but it is received only when it possesses the whole soul, and finds a seat and resting place in the inmost affection of the heart. Accordingly, either let them cease to boast of what they are not, in contempt of God; or let them show themselves disciples not unworthy of Christ their teacher. We have given the first place to the doctrine in which our religion is contained, since our salvation begins with it. But it must enter our heart and pass into our daily living, and so transform us into itself that it may not be unfruitful for us. The philosophers rightly burn with anger against, and reproachfully drive from their flock, those who when they profess an art that ought to be the mistress of life, turn it into sophistical chatter. With how much better reason, then, shall we detest these trifling Sophists who are content to roll the gospel on the tips of their tongues when its efficacy ought to penetrate the inmost affections of the heart, take its seat in the soul, and affect the whole man a hundred times more deeply than the cold exhortations of the philosophers!

5. Imperfection and endeavor of the Christian life

I do not insist that the moral life of a Christian man breathe nothing but the very gospel, yet this ought to be desired, and we must strive toward it. But I do not so strictly demand evangelical perfection that I would not acknowledge as a Christian one who has not yet attained it. For thus all would be excluded from the church, since no one is found who is not far removed from it, while many have advanced a little toward it whom it would nevertheless be unjust to cast away.

What then? Let that target be set before our eyes at which we are earnestly to aim. Let that goal be appointed toward which we should strive and struggle. For it is not lawful for you to divide things with God in such a manner that you undertake part of those things which are enjoined upon you by his Word but omit part, according to your own judgment. For in the first place, he everywhere commends integrity as the chief part of worshiping him [Gen. 17:1; Ps. 41:12; etc.]. By this word he means a sincere simplicity of mind, free from guile and feigning, the opposite of a double heart. It is as if it were said that the beginning of right living is spiritual, where the inner feeling of the mind is unfeignedly dedicated to God for the cultivation of holiness and righteousness.

But no one in this earthly prison of the body has sufficient strength to press on with due eagerness, and weakness so weighs down the greater number that, with wavering and limping and even creeping along the ground, they move at a feeble rate. Let each one of us, then, proceed according to the measure of his puny capacity and set out upon the journey we have begun. No one shall set out so inauspiciously as not daily to make some headway, though it be slight. Therefore, let us not cease so to act that we may make some unceasing progress in the way of the Lord. And let us not despair at the slightness of our success; for even though attainment may not correspond to desire, when today outstrips yesterday the effort is not lost. Only let us look toward our mark with sincere simplicity and aspire to our goal; not fondly flattering ourselves, nor excusing our own evil deeds, but with continuous effort striving toward this end: that we may surpass ourselves in goodness until we attain to goodness itself. It is this, indeed, which through the whole course of life we seek and follow. But we shall attain it only when we have cast off the weakness of the body, and are received into full fellowship with him.

CHAPTER VII
THE SUM OF THE CHRISTIAN LIFE:
THE DENIAL OF OURSELVES

1. We are not our own masters, but belong to God

Even though the law of the Lord provides the finest and best-disposed method of ordering a man's life, it seemed good to the Heavenly Teacher to shape his people by an even more explicit plan to that rule which he had set forth in the law. Here, then, is the beginning of this plan: the duty of believers is "to present their bodies to God as a living sacrifice, holy and acceptable to him," and in this consists the lawful worship of him [Rom. 12:1]. From this is derived the basis of the exhortation that "they be not conformed to the fashion of this world, but be transformed by the renewal of their minds, so that they may prove what is the will of God" [Rom. 12:2]. Now the great thing is this: we are consecrated and dedicated to God in order that we may thereafter think, speak, meditate, and do nothing except to his glory. For a sacred thing may not be applied to profane uses without marked injury to him.

If we, then, are not our own [cf. I Cor. 6:19] but the Lord's, it is clear what error we must flee, and whither we must direct all the acts of our life.

We are not our own: let not our reason nor our will, therefore, sway our plans and deeds. We are not our own: let us therefore not set it as our goal to seek what is expedient for us according to the flesh. We are not our own: insofar as we can, let us therefore forget ourselves and all that is ours.

Conversely, we are God's: let us therefore live for him and die for him. We are God's: let his wisdom and will therefore rule all our actions. We are God's: let all the parts of our life accordingly strive toward him as our only lawful goal [Rom. 14:8; cf. I Cor. 6:19]. O, how much has that man profited who, having been taught that he is not his own, has taken away dominion and rule from his own reason that he may yield it to God! For, as consulting our self-interest is the pestilence that most effectively leads to our destruction, so the sole haven of salvation is to be wise in nothing and to will nothing through ourselves but to follow the leading of the Lord alone.

Let this therefore be the first step, that a man depart from himself in order that he may apply the whole force of his ability in the service of the Lord. I call "service" not only what lies in obedience to God's Word but what turns the mind of man, empty of its own carnal sense, wholly to the bidding of God's Spirit. While it is the first entrance to life, all philosophers were ignorant of this transformation, which Paul calls "renewal of the mind" [Eph. 4:23]. For they set up reason alone as the ruling principle in man, and think that it alone should be listened to; to it alone, in short, they entrust the conduct of life. But the Christian philosophy bids reason give way to, submit and subject itself to, the Holy Spirit so that the man himself may no longer live but hear Christ living and reigning within him [Gal. 2:20].

2. Self-denial through devotion to God

From this also follows this second point: that we seek not the things that are ours but those which are of the Lord's will and will serve to advance his glory. This is also evidence of great progress: that, almost forgetful of ourselves, surely subordinating our self-concern, we try faithfully to devote our zeal to God and his commandments. For when Scripture bids us leave off self-concern, it not only erases from our minds the yearning to possess, the desire for power, and the favor of men, but it also uproots ambition and all craving for human glory and other more secret plagues. Accordingly, the Christian must surely be so disposed and minded that he feels within himself it is with God he has to deal throughout his life. In this way, as he will refer all he has to God's decision and judgment, so will he refer his whole intention of mind scrupulously to Him. For he who has learned to look to God in all things that he must do, at the same time avoids all vain thoughts. This, then, is that denial of self which Christ enjoins with such great earnestness upon his disciples at the outset of their service [cf. Matt. 16:24]. When it has once taken possession of their hearts, it leaves no place at all first either to pride, or arrogance, or ostentation; then either to avarice, or desire, or lasciviousness, or effeminacy, or to other evils that our self-love spawns [cf. II Tim. 3:2–5]. On the other hand, wherever denial of ourselves does not reign, there either the foulest vices rage without shame or if there is any semblance of virtue, it is vitiated by depraved lusting after glory. Show me a man, if you can, who, unless he has according to the commandment of the Lord renounced himself, would freely exercise goodness among men. For all who have not been possessed with this feeling have at least followed virtue for the sake of praise. Now those of the philosophers who at any time most strongly contended that virtue should be pursued for its own sake were puffed up with such great arrogance as to show they sought after virtue for no other reason than to have occasion for pride. Yet God is so displeased, both with those who court the popular breeze and with such swollen souls, as to declare that they have received their reward in this world [Matt. 6:2, 5, 16], and to make harlots and publicans nearer to the Kingdom of Heaven than are they [Matt. 21:31]. Yet we have still not clearly explained how many and how great are the obstacles that hinder man from a right course so long as he has not denied himself. For it was once truly said: "A world of vices is hidden in the soul of man." And you can find no other remedy than in denying yourself and giving up concern for yourself, and in turning your mind wholly to seek after those things which the Lord requires of you, and to seek them only because they are pleasing to him.

3. Self-renunciation according to Titus, Ch. 2

In another place, Paul more clearly, although briefly, delineates the individual parts of a well-ordered life. "The grace of God has appeared, bringing salvation to all men, training us to renounce irreligion and worldly passions and to live sober, upright, and godly lives, in the present age; awaiting our blessed hope, and the appearing of the glory of our great God and of our Savior Jesus Christ, who gave himself for us to redeem us from all iniquity and to purify for himself a people of his own who are zealous for good deeds" [Titus 2:11–14]. For, after he proffered the grace of God to hearten us, in order to pave the way for us to worship God truly he removed the two obstacles that chiefly hinder us: namely, ungodliness, to which by nature we are too much inclined; and second, worldly desires, which extend more widely. And by ungodliness, indeed, he not only means superstition but includes also whatever contends against the earnest fear of God. Worldly lusts are also equivalent to the passions of the flesh [cf. I John 2:16; Eph. 2:3; II Peter 2:18; Gal. 5:16; etc.]. Thus, with reference to both Tables of the Law, he commands us to put off our own nature and to deny whatever our reason and will dictate. Now he limits all actions of life to three parts: soberness, righteousness, and godliness. Of these, soberness

doubtless denotes chastity and temperance as well as a pure
and frugal use of temporal goods, and patience in poverty.
Now righteousness embraces all the duties of equity in order
that to each one be rendered what is his own [cf. Rom. 13:7].
There follows godliness, which joins us in true holiness with
God when we are separated from the iniquities of the world.
When these things are joined together by an inseparable bond,
they bring about complete perfection. But, nothing is more
difficult than, having bidden farewell to the reason of the flesh
and having bridled our desires—nay, having put them away—
to devote ourselves to God and our brethren, and to meditate,
amid earth's filth, upon the life of the angels. Consequently,
Paul, in order to extricate our minds from all snares, recalls
us to the hope of blessed immortality, reminding us that we
strive not in vain [cf. I Thess. 3:5]. For, as Christ our Redeemer
once appeared, so in his final coming he will show the fruit
of the salvation brought forth by him. In this way he scatters
all the allurements that becloud us and prevent us from as-
piring as we ought to heavenly glory. Nay, he teaches us to
travel as pilgrims in this world that our celestial heritage may
not perish or pass away.

4. Self-denial gives us the right attitude toward our fellow men

Now in these words we perceive that denial of self has regard
partly to men, partly, and chiefly, to God.

For when Scripture bids us act toward men so as to esteem
them above ourselves [Phil. 2:3], and in good faith to apply
ourselves wholly to doing them good [cf. Rom. 12:10], it gives
us commandments of which our mind is quite incapable unless
our mind be previously emptied of its natural feeling. For,
such is the blindness with which we all rush into self-love that
each one of us seems to himself to have just cause to be proud
of himself and to despise all others in comparison. If God has

conferred upon us anything of which we need not repent, relying upon it we immediately lift up our minds, and are not only puffed up but almost burst with pride. The very vices that infest us we take pains to hide from others, while we flatter ourselves with the pretense that they are slight and insignificant, and even sometimes embrace them as virtues. If others manifest the same endowments we admire in ourselves, or even superior ones, we spitefully belittle and revile these gifts in order to avoid yielding place to such persons. If there are any faults in others, not content with noting them with severe and sharp reproach, we hatefully exaggerate them. Hence arises such insolence that each one of us, as if exempt from the common lot, wishes to tower above the rest, and loftily and savagely abuses every mortal man, or at least looks down upon him as an inferior. The poor yield to the rich; the common folk, to the nobles; the servants, to their masters; the unlearned, to the educated. But there is no one who does not cherish within himself some opinion of his own pre-eminence.

Thus, each individual, by flattering himself, bears a kind of kingdom in his breast. For claiming as his own what pleases him, he censures the character and morals of others. But if this comes to the point of conflict, his venom bursts forth. For many obviously display some gentleness so long as they find everything sweet and pleasant. But just how many are there who will preserve this even tenor of modesty when they are pricked and irritated? There is no other remedy than to tear out from our inward parts this most deadly pestilence of love of strife and love of self, even as it is plucked out by Scriptural teaching. For thus we are instructed to remember that those talents which God has bestowed upon us are not our own goods but the free gifts of God; and any persons who become proud of them show their ungratefulness. "Who causes you to excel?" Paul asks. "If you have received all things, why do you boast as if they were not given to you?" [I Cor. 4:7].

Let us, then, unremittingly examining our faults, call ourselves back to humility. Thus nothing will remain in us to puff
us up; but there will be much occasion to be cast down. On
the other hand, we are bidden so to esteem and regard whatever gifts of God we see in other men that we may honor
those men in whom they reside. For it would be great depravity on our part to deprive them of that honor which the Lord
has bestowed upon them. But we are taught to overlook their
faults, certainly not flatteringly to cherish them; but not on
account of such faults to revile men whom we ought to cherish
with good will and honor. Thus it will come about that,
whatever man we deal with, we shall treat him not only
moderately and modestly but also cordially and as a friend.
You will never attain true gentleness except by one path: a
heart imbued with lowliness and with reverence for others.

5. Self-renunciation leads to proper helpfulness toward our neighbors

Now, in seeking to benefit one's neighbor, how difficult it is
to do one's duty! Unless you give up all thought of self and,
so to speak, get out of yourself, you will accomplish nothing
here. For how can you perform those works which Paul
teaches to be the works of love, unless you renounce yourself,
and give yourself wholly to others? "Love," he says, "is patient
and kind, not jealous or boastful, is not envious or puffed up,
does not seek its own, is not irritable," etc. [I Cor. 13: 4–5 p.].
If this is the one thing required—that we seek not what is our
own—still we shall do no little violence to nature, which so
inclines us to love of ourselves alone that it does not easily
allow us to neglect ourselves and our possessions in order to
look after another's good, nay, to yield willingly what is ours
by right and resign it to another. But Scripture, to lead us by
the hand to this, warns that whatever benefits we obtain from
the Lord have been entrusted to us on this condition: that

they be applied to the common good of the church. And therefore the lawful use of all benefits consists in a liberal and kindly sharing of them with others. No surer rule and no more valid exhortation to keep it could be devised than when we are taught that all the gifts we possess have been bestowed by God and entrusted to us on condition that they be distributed for our neighbors' benefit [cf. I Peter 4:10].

But Scripture goes even farther by comparing them to the powers with which the members of the human body are endowed [I Cor. 12:12 ff.]. No member has this power for itself nor applies it to its own private use; but each pours it out to the fellow members. Nor does it take any profit from its power except what proceeds from the common advantage of the whole body. So, too, whatever a godly man can do he ought to be able to do for his brothers, providing for himself in no way other than to have his mind intent upon the common upbuilding of the church. Let this, therefore, be our rule for generosity and beneficence: We are the stewards of everything God has conferred on us by which we are able to help our neighbor, and are required to render account of our stewardship. Moreover, the only right stewardship is that which is tested by the rule of love. Thus it will come about that we shall not only join zeal for another's benefit with care for our own advantage, but shall subordinate the latter to the former.

And lest perhaps we should not realize that this is the rule for the proper management of all gifts we have received from God, he also in early times applied it to the least gifts of his generosity. For he commanded that the first fruits be brought to him by which the people were to testify that it was unlawful to accept for themselves any enjoyment of benefits not previously consecrated to him [Ex. 23:19; cf. ch. 22:29, Vg.]. But if the gifts of God are only thus sanctified to us when we have dedicated them by our hand to the Author himself, that which does not savor of such dedication is clearly a corrupt abuse. Yet you wish to strive in vain to enrich the Lord by sharing

your possessions; since, then, your generosity cannot extend
to him, you must, as the prophet says, practice it toward the
saints on earth [Ps. 16:2–3]. And alms are compared to holy
sacrifices so as to correspond now to those requirements of
the law [Heb. 13:16].

6. Love of neighbor is not dependent upon manner of men but looks to God

Furthermore, not to grow weary in well-doing [Gal. 6:9],
which otherwise must happen immediately, we ought to add
that other idea which the apostle mentions: "Love is patient
. . . and is not irritable" [1 Cor. 13:4–5]. The Lord commands
all men without exception "to do good" [Heb. 13:16]. Yet the
great part of them are most unworthy if they be judged by
their own merit. But here Scripture helps in the best way when
it teaches that we are not to consider that men merit of themselves but to look upon the image of God in all men, to which
we owe all honor and love. However, it is among members
of the household of faith that this same image is more carefully
to be noted [Gal. 6:10], insofar as it has been renewed and
restored through the Spirit of Christ. Therefore, whatever
man you meet who needs your aid, you have no reason to
refuse to help him. Say, "He is a stranger"; but the Lord has
given him a mark that ought to be familiar to you, by virtue
of the fact that he forbids you to despise your own flesh [Isa.
58:7, Vg.]. Say, "He is contemptible and worthless"; but the
Lord shows him to be one to whom he has deigned to give
the beauty of his image. Say that you owe nothing for any
service of his; but God, as it were, has put him in his own
place in order that you may recognize toward him the many
and great benefits with which God has bound you to himself.
Say that he does not deserve even your least effort for his
sake; but the image of God, which recommends him to you,
is worthy of your giving yourself and all your possessions.

Now if he has not only deserved no good at your hand, but has also provoked you by unjust acts and curses, not even this is just reason why you should cease to embrace him in love and to perform the duties of love on his behalf [Matt. 6:14; 18:35; Luke 17:3]. You will say, "He has deserved something far different of me." Yet what has the Lord deserved? While he bids you forgive this man for all sins he has committed against you, he would truly have them charged against himself. Assuredly there is but one way in which to achieve what is not merely difficult but utterly against human nature: to love those who hate us, to repay their evil deeds with benefits, to return blessings for reproaches [Matt. 5:44]. It is that we remember not to consider men's evil intention but to look upon the image of God in them, which cancels and effaces their transgressions, and with its beauty and dignity allures us to love and embrace them.

7. The outward work of love is not sufficient, but it is intention that counts!

This mortification, then, will take place in us only if we fulfill the duties of love. Now he who merely performs all the duties of love does not fulfill them, even though he overlooks none; but he, rather, fulfills them who does this from a sincere feeling of love. For it can happen that one who indeed discharges to the full all his obligations as far as outward duties are concerned is still all the while far away from the true way of discharging them. For you may see some who wish to seem very liberal and yet bestow nothing that they do not make reprehensible with a proud countenance or even insolent words. And in this tragic and unhappy age it has come to this pass, that most men give their alms contemptuously. Such depravity ought not to have been tolerable even among the pagans; of Christians something even more is required than to show a cheerful countenance and to render their duties pleasing with friendly words. First, they must put themselves in the place of him whom they see in need of their assistance, and pity his ill fortune as if they themselves experienced and bore it, so that they may be impelled by a feeling of mercy and humaneness to go to his aid just as to their own.

He who, thus disposed, proceeds to give help to his brethren will not corrupt his own duties by either arrogance or upbraiding. Furthermore, in giving benefits he will not despise his needy brother or enslave him as one indebted to himself. This would no more be reasonable than that we should either chide a sick member that the rest of the body labors to revive or consider it especially obligated to the remaining members because it has drawn more help to itself than it can repay. Now the sharing of tasks among members is believed to have nothing gratuitous about it but, rather, to be a payment of that which, due by the law of nature, it would be monstrous to refuse. Also, in this way it will come about that he who has discharged one kind of task will not think himself free, as commonly happens when a rich man, after he has given up something of his own, delegates to other men other burdens as having nothing at all to do with him. Rather, each man will so consider with himself that in all his greatness he is a debtor to his neighbors, and that he ought in exercising kindness toward them to set no other limit than the end of his resources; these, as widely as they are extended, ought to have their limits set according to the rule of love.

8. Self-denial toward God: devotion to his will!

Let us reiterate in fuller form the chief part of self-denial, which, as we have said, looks to God. And indeed, many things have been said about this already that it would be superfluous to repeat. It will be enough to show how it forms us to fair-mindedness and tolerance.

To begin with, then, in seeking either the convenience or the tranquillity of the present life, Scripture calls us to resign ourselves and all our possessions to the Lord's will, and to yield to him the desires of our hearts to be tamed and subjugated. To covet wealth and honors, to strive for authority, to heap up riches, to gather together all those follies which seem to make for magnificence and pomp, our lust is mad, our desire boundless. On the other hand, wonderful is our fear, wonderful our hatred, of poverty, lowly birth, and humble condition! And we are spurred to rid ourselves of them by every means. Hence we can see how uneasy in mind all those persons are who order their lives according to their own plan. We can see how artfully they strive—to the point of weariness—to obtain the goal of their ambition or avarice, while, on the other hand, avoiding poverty and a lowly condition.

In order not to be caught in such snares, godly men must hold to this path. First of all, let them neither desire nor hope for, nor contemplate, any other way of prospering than by the Lord's blessing. Upon this, then, let them safely and confidently throw themselves and rest. For however beautifully the flesh may seem to suffice unto itself, while it either strives by its own effort for honors and riches or relies upon its diligence, or is aided by the favor of men, yet it is certain that all these things are nothing; nor will we benefit at all, either by skill or by labor, except insofar as the Lord prospers them both. On the contrary, however, his blessing alone finds a way, even through all hindrances, to bring all things to a happy and favorable outcome for us; again, though entirely without it, to enable us to obtain some glory and opulence for ourselves (as we daily see impious men amassing great honors and riches), yet, inasmuch as those upon whom the curse of God rests taste not even the least particle of happiness, without this blessing we shall obtain nothing but what turns to our misfortune. For we ought by no means to desire what makes men more miserable.

9. Trust in God's blessing only

Therefore, suppose we believe that every means toward a prosperous and desirable outcome rests upon the blessing of God alone; and that, when this is absent, all sorts of misery and calamity dog us. It remains for us not greedily to strive after riches and honors—whether relying upon our own dexterity of wit or our own diligence, or depending upon the favor of men, or having confidence in vainly imagined fortune—but for us always to look to the Lord so that by his guidance we may be led to whatever lot he has provided for us. Thus it will first come to pass that we shall not dash out to seize upon riches and usurp honors through wickedness and by stratagems and evil arts, or greed, to the injury of our neighbors; but pursue only those enterprises which do not lead us away from innocence.

Who can hope for the help of a divine blessing amidst frauds, robberies, and other wicked arts? For as that blessing follows only him who thinks purely and acts rightly, thus it calls back from crooked thoughts and wicked actions all those who seek it. Then will a bridle be put on us that we may not burn with an immoderate desire to grow rich or ambitiously pant after honors. For with what shamelessness does a man trust that he will be helped by God to obtain those things which he desires contrary to God's Word? Away with the thought that God would abet with his blessing what he curses with his mouth! Lastly, if things do not go according to our wish and hope, we will still be restrained from impatience and loathing of our condition, whatever it may be. For we shall know that this is to murmur against God, by whose will riches and poverty, contempt and honor, are dispensed. To sum up, he who rests solely upon the blessing of God, as it has been here expressed, will neither strive with evil arts after those things which men customarily madly seek after, which he realizes will not profit him, nor will he, if things go well, give credit to himself or even to his diligence, or industry, or fortune. Rather, he will give God the credit as its Author. But if, while other men's affairs flourish, he makes but slight advancement, or even slips back, he will still bear his low estate with greater equanimity and moderation of mind than some profane person would bear a moderate success which merely does not correspond with his wish. For he indeed possesses a solace in which he may repose more peacefully than in the highest degree of wealth or power. Since this leads to his salvation, he considers that his affairs are ordained by the Lord. We see that David was so minded; while he follows God and gives himself over to his leading, he attests that he is like a child weaned from his mother's breast, and that he does not occupy himself with things too deep and wonderful for him [Ps. 131:1–2].

10. Self-denial helps us bear adversity

And for godly minds the peace and forbearance we have spoken of ought not to rest solely in this point; but it must also be extended to every occurrence to which the present life is subject. Therefore, he alone has duly denied himself who has so totally resigned himself to the Lord that he permits every part of his life to be governed by God's will. He who will be thus composed in mind, whatever happens, will not consider himself miserable nor complain of his lot with ill will toward God. How necessary this disposition is will appear if you weigh the many chance happenings to which we are subject. Various diseases repeatedly trouble us: now plague rages; now we are cruelly beset by the calamities of war; now ice and hail, consuming the year's expectation, lead to barrenness, which reduces us to poverty; wife, parents, children, neighbors are snatched away by death; our house is burned by fire. It is on account of these occurrences that men curse their life, loathe the day of their birth, abominate heaven and the light of day, rail against God, and as they are eloquent in blasphemy, accuse him of injustice and cruelty. But in these matters the believer must also look to God's kindness and truly fatherly indulgence. Accordingly, if he sees his house reduced to solitude by the removal of his kinsfolk, he will not indeed even then cease to bless the Lord, but rather will turn his attention to this thought: nevertheless, the grace of the Lord, which dwells in my house, will not leave it desolate. Or, if his crops are blasted by frost, or destroyed by ice, or beaten down with hail, and he sees famine threatening, yet he will not despair or bear a grudge against God, but will remain firm in this trust [cf. Ps. 78:47]: "Nevertheless we are in the Lord's protection, sheep brought up in his pastures" [Ps. 79:13]. The Lord will therefore supply food to us even in extreme barrenness. If he shall be afflicted by disease, he will not even then be so unmanned by the harshness of pain as to break forth into impatience and expostulate with God; but, by considering the righteousness and gentleness of God's chastening, he will recall himself to forbearance. In short, whatever happens, because he will know it ordained of God, he will undergo it with a peaceful and grateful mind so as not obstinately to resist the command of him into whose power he once for all surrendered himself and his every possession.

Especially let that foolish and most miserable consolation of the pagans be far away from the breast of the Christian man; to strengthen their minds against adversities, they charged these to fortune. Against fortune they considered it foolish to be angry because she was blind and unthinking, with unseeing eyes wounding the deserving and the undeserving at the same time. On the contrary, the rule of piety is that God's hand alone is the judge and governor of fortune, good or bad, and that it does not rush about with heedless force, but with most orderly justice deals out good as well as ill to us.

CHAPTER VIII
BEARING THE CROSS, A PART OF SELF-DENIAL

1. Christ's cross and ours

But it behooves the godly mind to climb still higher, to the height to which Christ calls his disciples: that each must bear his own cross [Matt. 16:24]. For whomever the Lord has adopted and deemed worthy of his fellowship ought to prepare themselves for a hard, toilsome, and unquiet life, crammed with very many and various kinds of evil. It is the Heavenly Father's will thus to exercise them so as to put his own children to a definite test. Beginning with Christ, his first-born, he follows this plan with all his children. For even though that Son was beloved above the rest, and in him the Father's mind was well pleased [Matt. 3:17 and 17:5], yet we see that far from being treated indulgently or softly, to speak the truth, while he dwelt on earth he was not only tried by a perpetual cross but his whole life was nothing but a sort of perpetual cross. The apostle notes the reason: that it behooved him to "learn obedience through what he suffered" [Heb. 5:8].

Why should we exempt ourselves, therefore, from the condition to which Christ our Head had to submit, especially since he submitted to it for our sake to show us an example of patience in himself? Therefore, the apostle teaches that God has destined all his children to the end that they be conformed to Christ [Rom. 8:29]. Hence also in harsh and difficult conditions, regarded as adverse and evil, a great comfort comes to us: we share Christ's sufferings in order that as he has passed from a labyrinth of all evils into heavenly glory, we may in like manner be led through various tribulations to the same glory [Acts 14:22]. So Paul himself elsewhere states: when we come to know the sharing of his sufferings, we at the same time grasp the power of his resurrection; and when we become like him in his death, we are thus made ready to share his glorious resurrection [Phil. 3:10–11]. How much can it do to soften all the bitterness of the cross, that the more we are afflicted with adversities, the more surely our fellowship with Christ is confirmed! By communion with him the very sufferings themselves not only become blessed to us but also help much in promoting our salvation.

2. The cross leads us to perfect trust in God's power

Besides this, our Lord had no need to undertake the bearing of the cross except to attest and prove his obedience to the Father. But as for us, there are many reasons why we must pass our lives under a continual cross. First, as we are by nature too inclined to attribute everything to our flesh—unless our feebleness be shown, as it were, to our eyes—we readily esteem our virtue above its due measure. And we do not doubt, whatever happens, that against all difficulties it will remain unbroken and unconquered. Hence we are lifted up into stupid and empty confidence in the flesh; and relying on it, we are then insolently proud against God himself, as if our own powers were sufficient without his grace.

He can best restrain this arrogance when he proves to us by experience not only the great incapacity but also the frailty under which we labor. Therefore, he afflicts us either with disgrace or poverty, or bereavement, or disease, or other calamities. Utterly unequal to bearing these, insofar as they touch us, we soon succumb to them. Thus humbled, we learn to call upon his power, which alone makes us stand fast under the weight of afflictions. But even the most holy persons, however much they may recognize that they stand not through their own strength but through God's grace, are too sure of their own fortitude and constancy unless by the testing of the cross he brings them into a deeper knowledge of himself. This complacency even stole upon David: "In my tranquillity I said, 'I shall never be moved.' O Jehovah, by thy favor thou hadst established strength for my mountain; thou didst hide thy face, I was dismayed" [Ps. 30:6–7]. For he confesses that in prosperity his senses had been so benumbed with sluggishness that, neglecting God's grace, upon which he ought to have depended, he so relied upon himself as to promise himself he could ever stand fast. If this happened to so great a prophet, what one of us should not be afraid and take care?

In peaceful times, then, they preened themselves on their great constancy and patience, only to learn when humbled by adversity that all this was hypocrisy. Believers, warned, I say, by such proofs of their diseases, advance toward humility and so, sloughing off perverse confidence in the flesh, betake themselves to God's grace. Now when they have betaken themselves there they experience the presence of a divine power in which they have protection enough and to spare.

3. The cross permits us to experience God's faithfulness and gives us hope for the future

And this is what Paul teaches: "Tribulations produce patience; and patience, tried character" [Rom. 5:3–4, cf. Vg.]. That God has promised to be with believers in tribulation [cf. II Cor. 1:4] they experience to be true, while, supported by his hand, they patiently endure—an endurance quite unattainable by their own effort. The saints, therefore, through forbearance experience the fact that God, when there is need, provides the assistance that he has promised. Thence, also, is their hope strengthened, inasmuch as it would be the height of ingratitude not to expect that in time to come God's truthfulness will be as constant and firm as they have already experienced it to be. Now we see how many good things, interwoven, spring from the cross. For, overturning that good opinion which we falsely entertain concerning our own strength, and unmasking our hypocrisy, which affords us delight, the cross strikes at our perilous confidence in the flesh. It teaches us, thus humbled, to rest upon God alone, with the result that we do not faint or yield. Hope, moreover, follows victory insofar as the Lord, by performing what he has promised, establishes his truth for the time to come. Even if these were the only reasons, it plainly appears how much we need the practice of bearing the cross.

And it is of no slight importance for you to be cleansed of your blind love of self that you may be made more nearly aware of your incapacity; to feel your own incapacity that you may learn to distrust yourself; to distrust yourself that you may transfer your trust to God; to rest with a trustful heart in God that, relying upon his help, you may persevere unconquered to the end; to take your stand in his grace that you may comprehend the truth of his promises; to have unquestioned certainty of his promises that your hope may thereby be strengthened.

4. The cross trains us to patience and obedience

The Lord also has another purpose for afflicting his people: to test their patience and to instruct them to obedience. Not that they can manifest any other obedience to him save what he has given them. But it so pleases him by unmistakable proofs to make manifest and clear the graces which he has conferred upon the saints, that these may not lie idle, hidden within. Therefore, by bringing into the open the power and constancy to forbear, with which he has endowed his servants, he is said to test their patience. From this arise those expressions: that God tried Abraham, and proved his piety from the fact that he did not refuse to sacrifice his one and only son [Gen. 22:1,12]. Therefore, Peter likewise teaches that our faith is proved by tribulations as gold is tested in a fiery furnace [I Peter 1:7]. For who would say it is not expedient that the most excellent gift of patience, which the believer has received from his God, be put to use that it may be certain and manifest? Nor will men otherwise ever esteem it as it deserves.

But if God himself does right in providing occasion to stir up those virtues which he has conferred upon his believers in order that they may not be hidden in obscurity—nay, lie useless and pass away—the afflictions of the saints, without which they would have no forbearance, are amply justified. They are also, I assert, instructed by the cross to obey, because thus they are taught to live not according to their own whim but according to God's will. Obviously, if everything went according to their own liking, they would not know what it is to follow God. And Seneca recalls that it was an old proverb, in exhorting any man to endure adversities, to say, "Follow God." By this the ancients hinted, obviously, that a man truly submitted to God's yoke only when he yielded his hand and back to His rod. But if it is most proper that we should prove ourselves obedient to our Heavenly Father in all things, we must surely not refuse to have him accustom us in every way to render obedience to him.

5. The cross as medicine

Still we do not see how necessary this obedience is to us unless we consider at the same time how great is the wanton impulse of our flesh to shake off God's yoke if we even for a moment softly and indulgently treat that impulse. For the same thing happens to it that happens to mettlesome horses. If they are fattened in idleness for some days, they cannot afterward be tamed for their high spirits; nor do they recognize their rider, whose command they previously obeyed. And what God complains of in the Israelites is continually in us: fattened and made flabby, we kick against him who has fed and nourished us [Deut. 32:15]. Indeed, God's beneficence ought to have allured us to esteem and love his goodness. But inasmuch as our ill will is such that we are, instead, repeatedly corrupted by his indulgence, it is most necessary that we be restrained by some discipline in order that we may not jump into such wantonness. Thus, lest in the unmeasured abundance of our riches we go wild; lest, puffed up with honors, we become proud; lest, swollen with other good things—either of the soul or of the body, or of fortune—we grow haughty, the Lord himself, according as he sees it expedient, confronts us and subjects and restrains our unrestrained flesh with the remedy of the cross. And this he does in various ways in accordance with what is healthful for each man. For not all of us suffer in equal degree from the same diseases or, on that account, need the same harsh cure. From this it is to be seen that some are tried by one kind of cross, others by another. But since the heavenly physician treats some more gently but cleanses others by harsher remedies, while he wills to provide for the health of all, he yet leaves no one free and untouched, because he knows that all, to a man, are diseased.

6. The cross as fatherly chastisement

Besides this, it is needful that our most merciful Father should not only anticipate our weakness but also often correct past transgressions so that he may keep us in lawful obedience to himself. Accordingly, whenever we are afflicted, remembrance of our past life ought immediately to come to mind; so we shall doubtless find that we have committed something deserving this sort of chastisement. And yet, exhortation to forbearance is not to be based principally upon the recognition of sin. For Scripture furnishes a far better conception when it says that the Lord chastens us by adversities "so that we may not be condemned along with the world" [I Cor. 11:32]. Therefore, also, in the very harshness of tribulations we must recognize the kindness and generosity of our Father toward us, since he does not even then cease to promote our salvation. For he afflicts us not to ruin or destroy us but, rather, to free us from the condemnation of the world. That thought will lead us to what Scripture teaches in another place: "My son, do not despise the Lord's discipline, or grow weary when he reproves you. For whom God loves, he rebukes, and embraces as a father his son" [Prov. 3:11–12 p.]. When we recognize the Father's rod, is it not our duty to show ourselves obedient and teachable children rather than, in arrogance, to imitate desperate men who have become hardened in their evil deeds? When we have fallen away from him, God destroys us unless by reproof he recalls us. Thus he rightly says that if we are without discipline we are illegitimate children, not sons [Heb. 12:8]. We are, then, most perverse if when he declares his benevolence to us and the care that he takes for our salvation, we cannot bear him. Scripture teaches that this is the difference between unbelievers and believers: the former, like slaves of inveterate and double-dyed wickedness, with chastisement become only worse and more obstinate. But the latter, like freeborn sons, attain repentance. Now you must choose in which group you would prefer to be numbered. But since we have spoken concerning this matter elsewhere, content with a brief reference, I shall stop here.

7. Suffering for righteousness' sake

Now, to suffer persecution for righteousness' sake is a singular comfort. For it ought to occur to us how much honor God bestows upon us in thus furnishing us with the special badge of his soldiery. I say that not only they who labor for the defense of the gospel but they who in any way maintain the cause of righteousness suffer persecution for righteousness. Therefore, whether in declaring God's truth against Satan's falsehoods or in taking up the protection of the good and the innocent against the wrongs of the wicked, we must undergo the offenses and hatred of the world, which may imperil either our life, our fortunes, or our honor. Let us not grieve or be troubled in thus far devoting our efforts to God, or count ourselves miserable in those matters in which he has with his own lips declared us blessed [Matt. 5:10]. Even poverty, if it be judged in itself, is misery; likewise exile, contempt, prison, disgrace; finally, death itself is the ultimate of all calamities. But when the favor of our God breathes upon us, every one of these things turns into happiness for us. We ought accordingly to be content with the testimony of Christ rather than with the false estimation of the flesh. So it will come about that we shall rejoice after the apostle's example, "whenever he will count us worthy to suffer dishonor for his name" [Acts 5:41 p.]. What then? If, being innocent and of good conscience, we are stripped of our possessions by the wickedness of impious folk, we are indeed reduced to penury among men. But in God's presence in heaven our true riches are thus increased. If we are cast out of our own house, then we will be the more intimately received into God's family. If we are vexed and despised, we but take all the firmer root in Christ. If we are branded with disgrace and ignominy, we but have a fuller place in the Kingdom of God. If we are slain, entrance into the blessed life will thus be open to us. Let us be ashamed to esteem less than the shadowy and fleeting allurements of the

present life, those things on which the Lord has set so great
a value.

8. Suffering under the cross, the Christian finds consolation in God

Scripture, then, by these and like warnings gives us abundant
comfort in either the disgrace or the calamity we bear for the
sake of defending righteousness. Consequently, we are too
ungrateful if we do not willingly and cheerfully undergo these
things at the Lord's hand; especially since this sort of cross
most properly belongs to believers, and by it Christ wills to
be glorified in us, just as Peter teaches [I Peter 4:12 ff.]. But
since for honorable natures to suffer disgrace is harsher than
a hundred deaths, Paul specifically warns us we shall suffer
not only persecutions but also reproaches because we hope
in the living God [I Tim. 4:10]. Thus, in another passage he
bids us walk after his example through ill repute and good
repute [II Cor. 6:8].

Yet such a cheerfulness is not required of us as to remove
all feeling of bitterness and pain. Otherwise, in the cross there
would be no forbearance of the saints unless they were tor-
mented by pain and anguished by trouble. If there were no
harshness in poverty, no torment in diseases, no sting in disgrace,
no dread in death—what fortitude or moderation would there
be in bearing them with indifference? But since each of these,
with an inborn bitterness, by its very nature bites the hearts of
us all, the fortitude of the believing man is brought to light
if—tried by the feeling of such bitterness—however grievously
he is troubled with it, yet valiantly resisting, he surmounts it.
Here his forbearance reveals itself: if sharply pricked he is
still restrained by the fear of God from breaking into any
intemperate act. Here his cheerfulness shines if, wounded by
sorrow and grief, he rests in the spiritual consolation of God.

9. The Christian, unlike the Stoic, gives expression to his pain and sorrow

This struggle which believers when they strive for patience and moderation maintain against the natural feeling of sorrow is fittingly described by Paul in these words: "We are pressed in every way but not rendered anxious; we are afflicted but not left destitute; we endure persecution but in it are not deserted; we are cast down but do not perish" [II Cor. 4:8–9 p.]. You see that patiently to bear the cross is not to be utterly stupefied and to be deprived of all feeling of pain. It is not as the Stoics of old foolishly described "the great-souled man": one who, having cast off all human qualities, was affected equally by adversity and prosperity, by sad times and happy ones—nay, who like a stone was not affected at all. And what did this sublime wisdom profit them? They painted a likeness of forbearance that has never been found among men, and can never be realized. Rather, while they want to possess a forbearance too exact and precise, they have banished its power from human life.

Now, among the Christians there are also new Stoics, who count it depraved not only to groan and weep but also to be sad and care ridden. These paradoxes proceed, for the most part, from idle men who, exercising themselves more in speculation than in action, can do nothing but invent such paradoxes for us. Yet we have nothing to do with this iron philosophy which our Lord and Master has condemned not only by his word, but also by his example. For he groaned and wept both over his own and others' misfortunes. And he taught his disciples in the same way: "The world," he says, "will rejoice; but you will be sorrowful and will weep" [John 16:20 p.]. And that no one might turn it into a vice, he openly proclaimed, "Blessed are those who mourn" [Matt. 5:4]. No wonder! For if all weeping is condemned, what shall we judge concerning the Lord himself, from whose body tears of blood trickled down [Luke 22:44]? If all fear is branded as unbelief, how shall we account for that dread with which, we read, he was heavily stricken [Matt. 26:37; Mark 14:33]? If all sadness displeases us, how will it please us that he confesses his soul "sorrowful even to death" [Matt. 26:38]?

10. Real sorrow and real patience in conflict with each other

I decided to say this in order to recall godly minds from despair, lest, because they cannot cast off the natural feeling of sorrow, they forthwith renounce the pursuit of patience. This must necessarily happen to those who make patience into insensibility, and a valiant and constant man into a stock. For Scripture praises the saints for their forbearance when, so afflicted with harsh misfortune, they do not break or fall; so stabbed with bitterness, they are at the same time flooded with spiritual joy; so pressed by apprehension, they recover their breath, revived by God's consolation. In the meantime, their hearts still harbor a contradiction between their natural sense, which flees and dreads what it feels adverse to itself, and their disposition to godliness, which even through these difficulties presses toward obedience to the divine will. The Lord expresses this contradiction when he speaks to Peter as follows: "When you were young, you girded yourself and walked where you would. But when you become old . . . another will gird you and lead you where you do not wish to go" [John 21:18 p.]. It is unlikely that Peter, when it became necessary to glorify God through death, was drawn to it, unwilling and resisting. Otherwise, there would have been little praise for his martyrdom. But, even though he obeyed the divine command with the utmost fervor of heart, yet, because he had not put off his human nature, he was pulled apart by a double will. For while he contemplated that bloody death which he was to die, stricken with dread of it, he would gladly have escaped. On the other hand, when it came to his mind that he was called to it by God's command, having overcome and trampled his fear, he willingly and even cheerfully undertook it. This, therefore, we must try to do if we would be disciples of Christ, in order that our minds may be steeped in such reverence and obedience toward God as to be able to tame and subjugate to his command all contrary affections. Thus it will come to pass that, by whatever kind of cross we may be troubled, even in the greatest tribulations of mind, we shall firmly keep our patience. For the adversities themselves will have their own bitterness to gnaw at us; thus afflicted by disease, we shall both groan and be uneasy and pant after health; thus pressed by poverty, we shall be pricked by the arrows of care and sorrow; thus we shall be smitten by the pain of disgrace, contempt, injustice; thus at the funerals of our dear ones we shall weep the tears that are owed to our nature. But the conclusion will always be: the Lord so willed, therefore let us follow his will. Indeed, amid the very pricks of pain, amid groaning and tears, this thought must intervene: to incline our heart to bear cheerfully those things which have so moved it.

11. Patience according to philosophic and Christian understanding

Now, since we have taken the prime reason for bearing the cross from the contemplation of the divine will, we must define in a few words the difference between philosophic and Christian patience. Certainly, very few philosophers have climbed to such a height of reason as to understand that through afflictions we are tested by the hand of God, and to reckon that in this respect we must obey God. But they also advance no other reason than that it must be so. What else is this but to say that you must yield to God because it is vain for you to try to resist him? For if we obey God only because it is necessary, if we should be allowed to escape, we will cease to obey him. But Scripture bids us contemplate in the will of God something far different: namely, first righteousness and equity, then concern for our own salvation. Of this sort, then, are Christian exhortations to patience. Whether poverty or exile, or prison, or insult, or disease, or bereavement, or anything like them torture us, we must think that none of these things happens except by the will and providence of God, that he does nothing except with a well-ordered justice. What then? Do not our innumerable and daily offenses deserve to be chastised more severely and with heavier rods than the afflictions he lays upon us out of his kindness? Is it not perfectly fair that our flesh be tamed and made accustomed, as it were, to the yoke, lest it lustfully rage according to its own inward nature? Are not God's right and truth worth our trouble? But if God's undoubted equity appears in afflictions, we cannot either murmur or wrestle against it without iniquity. Now we do not hear that barren incantation, "We must yield because it is necessary," but a living and fully effective precept, "We must obey because it is unlawful to resist; we must bear patiently, since impatience would be insolence against God's righteousness."

Now, because that only is pleasing to us which we recognize to be for our salvation and good, our most merciful Father consoles us also in this respect when he asserts that in the very act of afflicting us with the cross he is providing for our salvation. But if it be clear that our afflictions are for our benefit, why should we not undergo them with a thankful and quiet mind?

Therefore, in patiently suffering these tribulations, we do not yield to necessity, but we consent for our own good. These thoughts, I say, bring it to pass that, however much in bearing the cross our minds are constrained by the natural feeling of bitterness, they are as much diffused with spiritual joy. From this, thanksgiving also follows, which cannot exist without joy; but if the praise of the Lord and thanksgiving can come forth only from a cheerful and happy heart—and there is nothing that ought to interrupt this in us—it thus is clear how necessary it is that the bitterness of the cross be tempered with spiritual joy.

CHAPTER IX
MEDITATION ON THE FUTURE LIFE

1. The vanity of this life

Whatever kind of tribulation presses upon us, we must ever look to this end: to accustom ourselves to contempt for the present life and to be aroused thereby to meditate upon the future life. For since God knows best how much we are inclined by nature to a brutish love of this world, he uses the fittest means to draw us back and to shake off our sluggishness, lest we cleave too tenaciously to that love. There is not one of us, indeed, who does not wish to seem throughout his life to aspire and strive after heavenly immortality. For it is a shame for us to be no better than brute beasts, whose condition would be no whit inferior to our own if there were not left to us hope of eternity after death. But if you examine the plans, the efforts, the deeds, of anyone, there you will find nothing else but earth. Now our blockishness arises from the fact that our minds, stunned by the empty dazzlement of riches, power, and honors, become so deadened that they can see no farther. The heart also, occupied with avarice, ambition, and lust, is so weighed down that it cannot rise up higher. In fine, the whole soul, enmeshed in the allurements of the flesh, seeks its happiness on earth. To counter this evil the Lord instructs his followers in the vanity of the present life by continual proof of its miseries. Therefore, that they may not promise themselves a deep and secure peace in it, he permits them often to be troubled and plagued either with wars or tumults, or robberies, or other injuries. That they may not pant with too great eagerness after fleeting and transient riches, or repose in those which they possess, he sometimes by exile, sometimes by barrenness of the earth, sometimes by fire, sometimes by other means, reduces them to poverty, or at least confines them to a moderate station. That they may not too complacently take delight in the goods of marriage, he either causes them to be troubled by the depravity of their wives or humbles them by evil offspring, or afflicts them with bereavement. But if, in all these matters, he is more indulgent toward them, yet, that they may not either be puffed up with vainglory or exult in self-assurance, he sets before their eyes, through diseases and perils, how unstable and fleeting are all the goods that are subject to mortality.

Then only do we rightly advance by the discipline of the cross, when we learn that this life, judged in itself, is troubled, turbulent, unhappy in countless ways, and in no respect clearly happy; that all those things which are judged to be its goods are uncertain, fleeting, vain, and vitiated by many intermingled evils. From this, at the same time, we conclude that in this life we are to seek and hope for nothing but struggle; when we think of our crown, we are to raise our eyes to heaven. For this we must believe: that the mind is never seriously aroused to desire and ponder the life to come unless it be previously imbued with contempt for the present life.

2. Our tendency to leave unnoticed the vanity of this life

Indeed, there is no middle ground between these two: either the world must become worthless to us or hold us bound by intemperate love of it. Accordingly, if we have any concern for eternity, we must strive diligently to strike off these evil fetters. Now, since the present life has very many allurements with which to entice us, and much show of pleasantness, grace, and sweetness wherewith to wheedle us, it is very much in our interest to be called away now and again so as not to be captivated by such panderings. What, then, I beg of you, would happen if we enjoyed here an enduring round of wealth and happiness, since we cannot, even with evil continually goading us, be sufficiently awakened to weigh the misery of this life?

That human life is like smoke [cf. Ps. 102:3] or shadow [cf. Ps. 102:11] is not only obvious to the learned, but even ordinary folk have no proverb more commonplace than this. And since they counted this something very profitable to know, they have couched it in many striking sayings. But there is almost nothing that we regard more negligently or remember less. For we undertake all things as if we were establishing immortality for ourselves on earth. If some corpse is being buried, or we walk among graves, because the likeness of death then meets our eyes, we, I confess, philosophize brilliantly concerning the vanity of this life. Yet even this we do not do consistently, for often all these things affect us not one bit. But when it happens, our philosophy is for the moment; it vanishes as soon as we turn our backs, and leaves not a trace of remembrance behind it. In the end, like applause in the theater for some pleasing spectacle, it evaporates. Forgetful not only of death but also of mortality itself, as if no inkling of it had ever reached us, we return to our thoughtless assurance of earthly immortality. If anyone in the meantime croaks the proverb: "Man is the creature of a day," we indeed admit it; but with no attention, so that the thought of perpetuity nonetheless remains fixed in our minds. Who, then, can deny that it is very much worth-while for all of us, I do not say to be admonished with words, but by all the experiences that can happen, to be convinced of the miserable condition of earthly life; inasmuch as, even when convinced, we scarcely cease to be stunned with a base and foolish admiration of it, as if it contained in itself the ultimate goal of good things. But if God has to instruct us, it is our duty, in turn, to listen to him calling us, shaking us out of our sluggishness, that, holding the world in contempt, we may strive with all our heart to meditate upon the life to come.

3. Gratitude for earthly life!

But let believers accustom themselves to a contempt of the present life that engenders no hatred of it or ingratitude against God. Indeed, this life, however crammed with infinite miseries it may be, is still rightly to be counted among those blessings of God which are not to be spurned. Therefore, if we recognize in it no divine benefit, we are already guilty of grave ingratitude toward God himself. For believers especially, this ought to be a testimony of divine benevolence, wholly destined, as it is, to promote their salvation. For before he shows us openly the inheritance of eternal glory, God wills by lesser proofs to show himself to be our Father. These are the benefits that are daily conferred on us by him. Since, therefore, this life serves us in understanding God's goodness, should we despise it as if it had no grain of good in itself? We must, then, become so disposed and minded that we count it among those gifts of divine generosity which are not at all to be rejected. For if testimonies of Scripture were lacking, and they are very many and very clear, nature itself also exhorts us to give thanks to the Lord because he has brought us into its light, granted us the use of it, and provided all the necessary means to preserve it.

And this is a much greater reason if in it we reflect that we are in preparation, so to speak, for the glory of the Heavenly Kingdom. For the Lord has ordained that those who are one day to be crowned in heaven should first undergo struggles on earth in order that they may not triumph until they have overcome the difficulties of war, and attained victory.

Then there is another reason: we begin in the present life, through various benefits, to taste the sweetness of the divine generosity in order to whet our hope and desire to seek after the full revelation of this. When we are certain that the earthly life we live is a gift of God's kindness, as we are beholden to him for it we ought to remember it and be thankful. Then we shall come in good time to consider its most unhappy condition in order that we may, indeed, be freed from too much desire of it, to which, as has been said, we are of ourselves inclined by nature.

4. The right longing for eternal life

Now whatever is taken away from the perverse love of this life ought to be added to the desire for a better one. I confess that those showed a very sound judgment who thought it the best thing not to be born, and the next best thing to die as quickly as possible [cf. Eccl. 4:2–3]. Since they were deprived of the light of God and true religion, what could they see in it that was not unhappy and repulsive? And they did not act without reason who celebrated the birthdays of their kindred with sorrow and tears, but their funeral rites with solemn joy. But they did this without profit because, bereft of the right teaching of faith, they did not see how something that is neither blessed nor desirable of itself can turn into something good for the devout. Thus in despair they brought their judgment to a close.

Let the aim of believers in judging mortal life, then, be that while they understand it to be of itself nothing but misery, they may with greater eagerness and dispatch betake themselves wholly to meditate upon that eternal life to come. When it comes to a comparison with the life to come, the present life can not only be safely neglected but, compared to the former, must be utterly despised and loathed. For, if heaven is our homeland, what else is the earth but our place of exile? If departure from the world is entry into life, what else is the world but a sepulcher? And what else is it for us to remain in life but to be immersed in death? If to be freed from the body is to be released into perfect freedom, what else is the body but a prison? If to enjoy the presence of God is the summit of happiness, is not to be without this, misery? But until we leave the world "we are away from the Lord" [II Cor. 5:6]. Therefore, if the earthly life be compared with the heavenly, it is doubtless to be at once despised and trampled under foot. Of course it is never to be hated except insofar as it holds us subject to sin; although not even hatred of that condition may ever properly be turned against life itself. In any case, it is still fitting for us to be so affected either by weariness or hatred of it that, desiring its end, we may also be prepared to abide in it at the Lord's pleasure, so that our weariness may be far from all murmuring and impatience. For it is like a sentry post at which the Lord has posted us, which we must hold until he recalls us. Paul, indeed, held too long in the bonds of the body, laments his lot and sighs with fervent desire for redemption [Rom. 7:24]. Nonetheless, that he may obey God's command he professes himself ready for either [Phil. 1:23–24]. For he acknowledges that he owes it to God to glorify his name whether through death or through life [Rom. 14:8]. But it is for God to determine what best conduces to his glory. Therefore, if it befits us to live and die to the Lord, let us leave to his decision the hour of our death and life, but in such a way that we may both burn with the zeal for death and be constant in meditation. But in comparison with the immortality to come, let us despise this life and long to renounce it, on account of bondage of sin, whenever it shall please the Lord.

5. Against the fear of death!

But monstrous it is that many who boast themselves Christians are gripped by such a great fear of death, rather than a desire for it, that they tremble at the least mention of it, as of something utterly dire and disastrous. Surely, it is no wonder if the natural awareness in us bristles with dread at the mention of our dissolution. But it is wholly unbearable that there is not in Christian hearts any light of piety to overcome and suppress that fear, whatever it is, by a greater consolation. For if we deem this unstable, defective, corruptible, fleeting, wasting, rotting tabernacle of our body to be so dissolved that it is soon renewed unto a firm, perfect, incorruptible, and finally heavenly glory, will not faith compel us ardently to seek what nature dreads? If we should think that through death we are recalled from exile to dwell in the fatherland, in the heavenly fatherland, would we get no comfort from this fact?

But, someone will object, there is nothing that does not crave to endure. To be sure, I agree; and so I maintain that we must have regard for the immortality to come, where a firm condition will be ours which nowhere appears on earth. For Paul very well teaches that believers eagerly hasten to death not because they want to be unclothed but because they long to be more fully clothed [II Cor. 5:2–3]. Shall the brute animals, and even inanimate creatures—even trees and stones—conscious of the emptiness of their present existence, long for the final day of resurrection, to be released from emptiness with the children of God [Rom. 8:19 ff.]; and shall we, endowed with the light of understanding, and above understanding illumined with the Spirit of God, when our very being is at stake, not lift our minds beyond this earthly decay?

But it is not my present purpose, nor is it the proper place, to dispute against this very great perversity. At the very beginning I stated that I had no intention of undertaking a detailed treatment of commonplaces. I would advise such timid minds to read Cyprian's treatise *On the Mortality*, unless they deserved to be sent off to the philosophers, that they may begin to blush when they see the contempt of death that the latter display.

Let us, however, consider this settled: that no one has made progress in the school of Christ who does not joyfully await the day of death and final resurrection. Paul, too, distinguishes all believers by this mark [Titus 2:13; cf. II Tim. 4:8], and Scripture habitually recalls us to it whenever it would set forth proof of perfect happiness. "Rejoice," says the Lord, "and raise your heads; for your redemption is drawing near" [Luke 21:28 p.]. Is it reasonable, I ask you, that what our Lord meant to be sufficient to arouse us to rejoicing and good cheer should engender nothing but sorrow and dismay? If this is so, why do we still boast of him as our Master? Let us, then, take hold of a sounder view, and even though the blind and stupid desire of the flesh resists, let us not hesitate to await the Lord's coming, not only with longing, but also with groaning and sighs, as the happiest thing of all. He will come to us as Redeemer, and rescuing us from this boundless abyss of all evils and miseries, he will lead us into that blessed inheritance of his life and glory.

6. The comfort prepared for believers by aspiration for the life to come

This is obvious: the entire company of believers, so long as they dwell on earth, must be "as sheep destined for the slaughter" [Rom. 8:36] to be conformed to Christ their Head. They would therefore have been desperately unhappy unless, with mind intent upon heaven, they had surmounted whatever is in this world, and passed beyond the present aspect of affairs [cf. I Cor. 15:19]. On the contrary, when they have once lifted their heads above everything earthly, even though they may see wicked men flourishing in wealth and honors, even though they may observe the latter enjoying deep peace, taking pride in the splendor and luxury of all their possessions, abounding with every delight—if, moreover, believers are troubled by the wickedness of these men, bear their arrogant insults, are robbed through their greed, or harried by any other sort of inordinate desire on their part—they will without difficulty bear up under such evils also. For before their eyes will be that day when the Lord will receive his faithful people into the peace of his Kingdom, "will wipe away every tear from their eyes" [Rev. 7:17; cf. Isa. 25:8], will clothe them with "a robe of glory . . . and rejoicing" [Ecclus. 6:31, EV], will feed them with the unspeakable sweetness of his delights, will elevate them to his sublime fellowship—in fine, will deign to make them sharers in his happiness. But those impious ones who have flourished on earth he will cast into utter disgrace; he will turn their delights into tortures, their laughter and mirth into weeping and gnashing of teeth; he will trouble their peace with the dire torment of conscience; he will punish their wantonness with unquenchable fire [cf. Isa. 66:24; Matt. 25:41; Mark 9:43, 46; Rev. 21:8]; he will also make them bow their heads in subjection to the godly, whose patience they have abused. For, as Paul testifies, this is righteousness: to grant rest to the unhappy and unjustly afflicted, to repay with affliction the wicked who afflict the godly, when the Lord Jesus is revealed from heaven [II Thess. 1:6–7].

This truly is our sole comfort. If it be taken away, either our minds must become despondent or, to our destruction, be captivated with the empty solace of this world. Even the prophet confesses that his steps had well-nigh wavered when he stopped too long to dwell upon the present prosperity of the wicked [Ps. 73:2–3], and he could not understand it until he entered God's sanctuary and gazed upon the ultimate end of the pious and the wicked [Ps. 73:17]. To conclude in a word: if believers' eyes are turned to the power of the resurrection, in their hearts the cross of Christ will at last triumph over the devil, flesh, sin, and wicked men.

CHAPTER X
HOW WE MUST USE THE PRESENT LIFE AND ITS HELPS

1. Double danger: mistaken strictness and mistaken laxity

By such elementary instruction, Scripture at the same time duly informs us what is the right use of earthly benefits—a matter not to be neglected in the ordering of our life. For if we are to live, we have also to use those helps necessary for living. And we also cannot avoid those things which seem to serve delight more than necessity. Therefore we must hold to a measure so as to use them with a clear conscience, whether for necessity or for delight. By his word the Lord lays down this measure when he teaches that the present life is for his people as a pilgrimage on which they are hastening toward the Heavenly Kingdom [Lev. 25:23; I Chron. 29:15; Ps. 39:13; 119:19; Heb. 11:8–10, 13–16; 13:14; I Peter 2:11]. If we must simply pass through this world, there is no doubt we ought to use its good things insofar as they help rather than hinder our course. Thus Paul rightly persuades us to use this world as if not using it; and to buy goods with the same attitude as one sells them [I Cor. 7:31–30].

But because this topic is a slippery one and slopes on both sides into error, let us try to plant our feet where we may safely stand. There were some otherwise good and holy men who when they saw intemperance and wantonness, when not severely restrained, ever raging with unbridled excess, desired to correct this dangerous evil. This one plan occurred to them: they allowed man to use physical goods insofar as necessity required. A godly counsel indeed, but they were far too severe. For they would fetter consciences more tightly than does the Word of the Lord—a very dangerous thing. Now, to them necessity means to abstain from all things that they could do without; thus, according to them, it would scarcely be permitted to add any food at all to plain bread and water. And others are even more severe. We are told of Crates the Theban, that he cast all his goods into the sea; for he thought that unless they were destroyed, they would destroy him.

But many today, while they seek an excuse for the intemperance of the flesh in its use of external things, and while they would meanwhile pave the road to licentious indulgence, take for granted what I do not at all concede to them: that this freedom is not to be restrained by any limitation but to be left to every man's conscience to use as far as seems lawful to him. Certainly I admit that consciences neither ought to nor can be bound here to definite and precise legal formulas; but inasmuch as Scripture gives general rules for lawful use, we ought surely to limit our use in accordance with them.

2. The main principle

Let this be our principle: that the use of God's gifts is not wrongly directed when it is referred to that end to which the Author himself created and destined them for us, since he created them for our good, not for our ruin. Accordingly, no one will hold to a straighter path than he who diligently looks to this end. Now if we ponder to what end God created food, we shall find that he meant not only to provide for necessity but also for delight and good cheer. Thus the purpose of clothing, apart from necessity, was comeliness and decency. In grasses, trees, and fruits, apart from their various uses, there is beauty of appearance and pleasantness of odor [cf. Gen. 2:9]. For if this were not true, the prophet would not have reckoned them among the benefits of God, "that wine gladdens the heart of man, that oil makes his face shine" [Ps. 104:15 p.]. Scripture would not have reminded us repeatedly, in commending his kindness, that he gave all such things to men. And the natural qualities themselves of things demonstrate sufficiently to what end and extent we may enjoy them. Has the Lord clothed the flowers with the great beauty that greets our eyes, the sweetness of smell that is wafted upon our nostrils, and yet will it be unlawful for our eyes to be affected by that beauty, or our sense of smell by the sweetness of that odor? What? Did he not so distinguish colors as to make some more lovely than others? What? Did he not endow gold and silver, ivory and marble, with a loveliness that renders them more precious than other metals or stones? Did he not, in short, render many things attractive to us, apart from their necessary use?

3. A look at the Giver of the gift prevents narrow-mindedness and immoderation

Away, then, with that inhuman philosophy which, while conceding only a necessary use of creatures, not only malignantly deprives us of the lawful fruit of God's beneficence but cannot be practiced unless it robs a man of all his senses and degrades him to a block.

But no less diligently, on the other hand, we must resist the lust of the flesh, which, unless it is kept in order, overflows

without measure. And it has, as I have said, its own advo-
cates, who, under the pretext of the freedom conceded, permit
everything to it. First, one bridle is put upon it if it be deter-
mined that all things were created for us that we might
recognize the Author and give thanks for his kindness toward
us. Where is your thanksgiving if you so gorge yourself with
banqueting or wine that you either become stupid or are
rendered useless for the duties of piety and of your calling?
Where is your recognition of God if your flesh boiling over
with excessive abundance into vile lust infects the mind with
its impurity so that you cannot discern anything that is right
and honorable? Where is our gratefulness toward God for
our clothing if in the sumptuousness of our apparel we both
admire ourselves and despise others, if with its elegance and
glitter we prepare ourselves for shameless conduct? Where
is our recognition of God if our minds be fixed upon the
splendor of our apparel? For many so enslave all their senses
to delights that the mind lies overwhelmed. Many are so
delighted with marble, gold, and pictures that they become
marble, they turn, as it were, into metals and are like painted
figures. The smell of the kitchen or the sweetness of its odors
so stupefies others that they are unable to smell anything
spiritual. The same thing is also to be seen in other matters.
Therefore, clearly, leave to abuse God's gifts must be somewhat curbed, and Paul's rule is confirmed: that we should
"make no provision for the flesh, to gratify its desires" [Rom.
13:14], for if we yield too much to these, they boil up without
measure or control.

4. Aspiration to eternal life also determines aright our outward conduct of life

But there is no surer or more direct course than that which
we receive from contempt of the present life and meditation

upon heavenly immortality. For from this two rules follow: those who use this world should be so affected as if they did not use it; those who marry, as if they did not marry; those who buy, as if they did not buy, just as Paul enjoins [I Cor. 7:29–31]. The other rule is that they should know how to bear poverty peaceably and patiently, as well as to bear abundance moderately. He who bids you use this world as if you used it not destroys not only the intemperance of gluttony in food and drink, and excessive indulgence at table, in buildings and clothing, ambition, pride, arrogance, and overfastidiousness, but also all care and inclination that either diverts or hinders you from thought of the heavenly life and zeal to cultivate the soul. Long ago Cato truly said: "There is great care about dress, but great carelessness about virtue." To use the old proverb: those who are much occupied with the care of the body are for the most part careless about their own souls.

Therefore, even though the freedom of believers in external matters is not to be restricted to a fixed formula, yet it is surely subject to this law: to indulge oneself as little as possible; but, on the contrary, with unflagging effort of mind to insist upon cutting off all show of superfluous wealth, not to mention licentiousness, and diligently to guard against turning helps into hindrances.

5. Frugality, earthly possessions held in trust

The second rule will be: they who have narrow and slender resources should know how to go without things patiently, lest they be troubled by an immoderate desire for them. If they keep this rule of moderation, they will make considerable progress in the Lord's school. So, too, they who have not progressed, in some degree at least, in this respect have scarcely anything to prove them disciples of Christ. For besides the fact that most other vices accompany the desire for earthly things, he who bears poverty impatiently also when in prosperity commonly betrays the contrary disease. This is my point: he who is ashamed of mean clothing will boast of costly clothing; he who, not content with a slender meal, is troubled by the desire for a more elegant one will also intemperately abuse those elegances if they fall to his lot. He who will bear reluctantly, and with a troubled mind, his deprivation and humble condition if he be advanced to honors, will by no means abstain from arrogance. To this end, then, let all those for whom the pursuit of piety is not a pretense strive to learn, by the Apostle's example, how to be filled and to hunger, to abound and to suffer want [Phil. 4:12].

Besides, Scripture has a third rule with which to regulate the use of earthly things. Of it we said something when we discussed the precepts of love. It decrees that all those things were so given to us by the kindness of God, and so destined for our benefit, that they are, as it were, entrusted to us, and we must one day render account of them. Thus, therefore, we must so arrange it that this saying may continually resound in our ears: "Render account of your stewardship" [Luke 16:2]. At the same time let us remember by whom such reckoning is required: namely, him who has greatly commended abstinence, sobriety, frugality, and moderation, and has also abominated excess, pride, ostentation, and vanity; who approves no other distribution of good things than one joined with love; who has already condemned with his own lips all delights that draw man's spirit away from chastity and purity, or befog his mind.

6. The Lord's calling a basis of our way of life

Finally, this point is to be noted: the Lord bids each one of us in all life's actions to look to his calling. For he knows with

what great restlessness human nature flames, with what fick-
leness it is borne hither and thither, how its ambition longs
to embrace various things at once. Therefore, lest through
our stupidity and rashness everything be turned topsy-turvy,
he has appointed duties for every man in his particular way
of life. And that no one may thoughtlessly transgress his limits,
he has named these various kinds of living "callings." Therefore each individual has his own kind of living assigned to
him by the Lord as a sort of sentry post so that he may not
heedlessly wander about throughout life. Now, so necessary
is this distinction that all our actions are judged in his sight
by it, often indeed far otherwise than in the judgment of
human and philosophical reason. No deed is considered
more noble, even among philosophers, than to free one's
country from tyranny. Yet a private citizen who lays his hand
upon a tyrant is openly condemned by the heavenly judge
[I Sam. 24:7, 11; 26:9].

But I will not delay to list examples. It is enough if we
know that the Lord's calling is in everything the beginning
and foundation of well-doing. And if there is anyone who
will not direct himself to it, he will never hold to the straight
path in his duties. Perhaps, sometimes, he could contrive
something laudable in appearance; but whatever it may be
in the eyes of men, it will be rejected before God's throne.
Besides, there will be no harmony among the several parts
of his life. Accordingly, your life will then be best ordered
when it is directed to this goal. For no one, impelled by his
own rashness, will attempt more than his calling will permit,
because he will know that it is not lawful to exceed its bounds.
A man of obscure station will lead a private life ungrudgingly
so as not to leave the rank in which he has been placed by
God. Again, it will be no slight relief from cares, labors,
troubles, and other burdens for a man to know that God is
his guide in all these things. The magistrate will discharge
his functions more willingly; the head of the household will

confine himself to his duty; each man will bear and swallow the discomforts, vexations, weariness, and anxieties in his way of life, when he has been persuaded that the burden was laid upon him by God. From this will arise also a singular consolation: that no task will be so sordid and base, provided you obey your calling in it, that it will not shine and be reckoned very precious in God's sight.

III

Calvin's Civic Spirituality of Sanctification

Coming of age in the developed twenty-first-century world includes learning about cosmic emergence and biological evolution, along with gaining a historicist imagination together with an acceptance of pluralism. A realistic appreciation of Calvin and the spirituality mediated by his theology requires appreciation of the differences of pre-Enlightenment ideas from those of today. Yet many of his convictions stimulate deeper transcultural resonance. For example, an eschatological horizon cannot mean that the world is not our home, since human existence evolved precisely as a function of this world: The world is our home, and we cannot despise earthly existence. Contempt for human life is in fact a planetary disease. A person committed to Jesus Christ today cannot easily imagine that Jesus's suffering stands for God's disciplining human beings. The controversies over predestination were so anthropomorphic in their rudimentary premises that entering them in those terms leads only to misunderstanding the character of faith and to ultimate frustration. One has to approach Calvin's often strong and clear language with a willingness to recognize its historicity and to look for deeper analogies with present-day experience rather than with one-to-one correspondence.

The distinction between the historical interpretation within the context of the past and its relevance for life today will seem to many like a license for a free-ranging imagination. But present-day receptions of Calvin have to appeal to the cultures of the receivers. And no single interpretation fits all. The interpretations offered here should not be considered peculiar or idiosyncratic but rather as attempts to bring forward those deeper analogies. These meanings spring from a dual respect for Calvin in his historical context and the realities of persons or groups trying to make Christian sense out of life in today's world. The six dimensions of Calvin's spirituality that are used to show his relevance for spirituality in today's world do not mean that we should shrink his thought; we must let it open up new possibilities.

Sense of Identity

A first characteristic of a spirituality schooled by Calvin's writing may be described as including a strong sense of identity springing from his theology of election and providence.[1] This quality, perhaps typical of the late Middle Ages, stands out today against the background of various forms of experiencing the radical contingency of life and a common loss of an overarching metaphysical perspective. Today's breadth of information seems to be accompanied by a lack of synthesis and depth. Calvin's sense of the absolute sovereignty of God, the all-embracing character of God's providence and governance of the world, and his view of God's will extending to each particular event, together, go well beyond a confidence that the world as a whole has coherent meaning. They descend, so to speak, to each one's personal existence; they bestow a sense of individual personhood that is fastly grounded. In the face of the randomness that seems to be written into the very fabric of space-time, God is still God, and the creator wills each one's being. This assurance, in other words, does not remain focused on the universe, the world, or society but descends to the consciousness of the individual person and provides a sense that one's being in the universe has meaning because of God's direct relationship to it. God intended it from the beginning and intends it now.[2]

This experiential dimension of Christian spirituality consistently shows itself across Christian tradition, but, most frequently, it finds expression as mediated by the person of Jesus Christ and in the doctrine of salvation. The experience of sin and moral depravity consistently defines part of the dilemma of human existence to which Christianity responds. Grace means forgiveness of sinful humankind and all individual persons, even in their moral failure. Calvin's Christian theology includes this, but his doctrine of God as absolute transcendent creator also embraces every aspect of what transpires on earth. Moreover, one cannot separate God's creating presence from God's love.[3] God's all-encompassing reality and all-embracing presence in power and love cannot be imagined, for the imagination immediately translates into some version of a human transaction and competing interests. God remains an absolute mystery, but not completely hidden, for Calvin positively refers to God's radiant "glory." This God as Presence can be experienced, and that encounter overflows into a basic trust and ratification of the self which carries meaning that can penetrate a barren, objectified, and secularized universe. As Troeltsch put it, a Christian in Calvin's world is "filled with a deep consciousness of his own value as a person, with the high sense of a Divine Mission to the world, of being mercifully privileged among thousands, and in possession of an immeasurable responsibility."[4] The point here is that Calvin's theocentrism, his overpowering sense of God as the creator of all, helps us to transcend reading the Christian message in competitive terms of some saved and others not. It locates the most basic place where God and the human connect in a universal metaphysical way as being within God's loving and creating will. The deep logic of God's sovereignty implies that God's saving activity reaches out to all and establishes their sacred identity.[5]

A Sense of an Eschatological Horizon

Christian spirituality rarely lacks some form of the idea of eschatology. John Cassian rendered it in teleological terms and saw it as the framework governing monastic existence. And Calvin used language not alien to the monks: "[W]e must ever look to this end: to accustom ourselves to contempt for the present life and . . . to meditate upon the future life" (3.9.1). Calvin speaks with metaphysical intent; he acknowledges death and hopes for eternal life. But this horizon had a considerably different effect on everyday life in Geneva and on life today from its construal in a monastic setting. Confidence in the victory of Christ and the promise of resurrection changes one's orientation toward earthly life. This new perspective liberates a person from the ultimacy of the fears of everyday life and the obstacles to human freedom.[6] An eschatological perspective frees the tragedies of human existence from their tyranny over the human imagination; the negatives of existence can in the end be rendered positive.[7] This does not make life easy. Calvin's eschatological imagination distances him from an escapist spirituality. To the contrary, it generates freedom for social engagement.[8]

One can begin to see how this works based on the previous consideration of the sovereignty of God and the conviction that God relates to the world with benevolent and loving favor. In this context an eschatological outlook absorbs into itself everyday personal and social existence in the world.

Whatever the concrete world of the person of faith may look like, an eschatological horizon can transform the depth and the breadth of its ultimate meaning.

In terms of depth, first, the "eschatological" does not refer to a time and place up ahead but to the transcendent depth of being itself. The *eschaton* refers to God's sphere, and it transcends space and time. It means "ultimate" rather than "last." As John Zizioulas puts it, the eschatological does not refer only to a "not yet" reality in an absolute future but to "a state of existence (which) confronts history already now with *a presence from beyond history*."[9] The eschatological consists of God's being present to and within being and suffusing it with a meaning that transcends time. This metaphysical status becomes liberating when it breaks into consciousness to transform a person's awareness of the status of the world, the self, and his or her place in it.

This new consciousness includes a second dimension: It gives new meaning to the whole of reality, the whole universe, and each thing in it, so that all the actual lateral relationships that attach a person to the world also change in significance. More will be said about these relationships in the last section of this reflection. But the accent here falls on the transformed and transforming meaning resulting from an eschatological perspective. It does not refer to a projected end of the world but to the all-encompassing "divine milieu," as Pierre Teilhard de Chardin called this depth dimension of spirituality. But at the same time, eschatology does transform the meaning of time. The eschatological does not mean a state of affairs but rather the ontological condition of finite reality and the consciousness that arises when one encounters it. "The eschatological hope is the conviction that the eternal will of God will carry to completion the work which it has begun. . . ."[10] The more one reflects on the role of the future in human consciousness, not a specific future but the open horizon of possibility, the more the meaning of this feature of Calvin's eschatology will grow in consequence.

A Sense of Personal Responsibility

The consideration of identity already broached this theme of being called to service. Each person's actual historical identity to a large extent consists of the abilities and talents that make up each one's character. Connecting the contingent bundle of gifts and relationships that have been assembled by evolution and that constitute each individual to the creating will and presence of God seems like an impossible challenge. Too much conflict and waste are attached to every positive gain. But within that mystery, recognition of God's creating communicates a sense of individual importance that an objective scientific understanding of the individual completely lacks. Coming to an awareness of one's relationship with God arises out of asking the question of the reason for each one's personal existence. The question includes an implicit quest to find that reason and live according to it. Calvin had a strong sense of God-given purpose for every individual thing.

But the seriousness of "purpose" in Calvin extends further through his conception of vocation. This too flows from the scope of his conception of the particular will of God. God has planned each person's vocation. It follows that living responsibly within one's family and work plays out God's role for each individual. This view of being called to service in society fits or incorporates within itself the doctrine of growth in sanctification. If the will of God embraces the whole of each person's life, it includes what each person does in the particularities of how he or she does it. People grow in their closeness to God as they go about their role in society and give witness to God's glory.

This conviction appears almost completely counterintuitive in present-day secular culture, where religion has become private and spirituality in any deep or practical sense has been pushed to the margins of everyday life. To actually find a job that is spiritually fulfilling seems utterly idealistic and utopian in a pragmatic, objective, and instrumentalized bureaucratic workplace. This conception of Calvin, however, should not be dismissed as merely a function of a late medieval religious culture. It appears rather as a legitimate aspiration and a quiet norm for finding a kind of work that satisfies a spiritual need or revisioning what one actually does in a way that is creative of more than a salary. Work can also be saved metaphysically. Whether or not God has a predetermined particular will for each person, which seems less likely in an open process view of reality, God's general will for the well-being of each particular person accommodates the desire of the human spirit that what we do in life counts.

A Sense of Social Responsibility

One of the most far-reaching principles of Calvin's anthropology and thus of the spiritual life finds expression in the idea of stewardship. Recall what this principle says: "that all those things [the gifts of creation] were so given to us by the kindness of God, and so destined for our benefit, that they are, as it were, entrusted to us, and we must one day render account of them" (3.10.5). This sentence had a straightforward meaning for Calvin: Human life consists in using the things of creation according to their intrinsic created purposes rather than according to our whims. He lifted up a principle from creation theology and applied it to what people should actually be doing. He thus announced a spiritual rationale for everyday activity. There are two things going on here, and they unite in a polar tension. On the one hand, since the intelligence and will of the Creator have provided the world with an intelligible structure, it makes spiritual sense to conform our decisions and usage to the will of the creator. On the other hand, human intelligence and freedom have given human beings a certain amount of control over ourselves and our social existence. Human beings are thus responsible for the world. The charge is great: "[We] must one day render an account" of our handling of the world in which we live.

Calvin could not have had any sense of the staggering importance that this principle has assumed in world history at the present time. Nor could he have imagined the nuance that the principle of stewardship has accrued. Given the relatively small numbers of human beings in the past and their relatively low level of technological development, the extent to which human beings could dominate, abuse, and injure nature was unthinkable. Even the way Calvin states it seems to assign to human beings too much power over creation and too little attention to human dependence on and need to listen to nature. But Calvin's theological vision communicates a spiritual responsibility that is constitutive of human freedom. It directly relates to the present-day human ability to attend to marginalized groups of people, or to ignore them, and to save or destroy the world. Calvin's sixteenth-century spiritual principle confronts each person today with the survival of the species. At this juncture of history, this responsibility defines our place in society, in the world, and in existence.

A spirituality of social responsibility also appears in Calvin's conception of the church within society. Calvin understood from the beginning when he designed the structure of the church at Geneva that it was to have a major role in the life of the city. And so it did. While there was no separation of church and state in his formula for Geneva, these powers were not coterminous; although church and civil government enjoyed distinct spheres, they overlapped in one society. What Calvin wanted for the church, he wanted for the city. He did not conceive the roles of church and civic authorities as moving forward along parallel rails; magistrates and ministers both looked after citizen behavior. The church had a function in society even as city government had a role in safeguarding or protecting the church. The role of the church as a holy community was to make society itself holy. However, he also recognized the complexity of relationships between these power centers. While he sketched an ideal which envisioned the church and government working in tandem, he did not naïvely require it. For instance, he acknowledged the early Christian's experience under Rome. Similarly, he personally understood that while the principle of state support and protection of ecclesial life and cooperation for the amelioration of the city would have been feasible in Geneva, it certainly would not have been conceivable in Calvin's home country of France at that time. This flexibility is precisely what makes Calvin's vision so incisive.

To be clear at this point, it would not be acceptable to think of the issue of the relationship between church and state in the terms that prevailed in Europe generally or Geneva in particular as applicable in twenty-first-century democracies. Today's global interdependence of nations, migration, increasing religious pluralism within nations, and separation of church and state all show that Calvin's Geneva is not exportable. But the other side of these issues consists of the relation of political engagement to the religious imagination, specifically that of Christianity. Calvin at least shows that participation in the world of social, political, and social construction is not alien to Christian spirituality. One finds no split between Christian ethics and life in the world; it is an ethic for life in the world.

Calvin proposes an ethical ideal for both the personal character of the Christian individual and for society in an all-embracing religious purpose that covers life in the world. The goal is the glory of God. On the level of the individual person, we've seen how each person has a place and a role in life. On a social level, the church brings its message and spiritual power to citizens as a group, and this has relevance for the public order. The church addresses moral conduct and, where possible, attends to people who have fallen through the cracks of social systems. Calvin held up civil service as a holy calling.[11] Many themes coalesce here: God's sovereignty, God's will, providence, election, human justification, progressive sanctification, calling, and use of creatures all point to Christian life as participation in the common good of human flourishing. As Troeltsch wrote, the follower of Calvin's spirituality is "drawn irresistibly into a whole-hearted absorption in the tasks of service to the world and to society, to a life of unceasing, penetrating, and formative labor."[12]

Reappropriating Absolute Respect for God's Will

God's sovereignty, God's will, and God's glory were omnipresent in Calvin's theological and spiritual imagination. Theocentrism, as opposed to anthropocentrism, provided the glasses through which he viewed reality. This in turn defined the fundamental attitude with which human beings should understand the world and themselves in it. It was a self-transcending vision; it presented a world out there to which human freedom should dedicate itself in order to be filled with God's values and conform to God's will. We do not live for ourselves; we live for God and God's glory. And the more we surrender to God's cause, the more we will be fulfilled. This correlates with Karl Barth's theocentric perspective: It is pure Calvin. And it holds out such an immense goal and value, absolute and eternal in principle, that it draws human freedom into itself absolutely.

But another way to introduce people to an absolute respect for God's will uses a more apologetic approach. "Apologetic" here means an appeal to current experience. It takes seriously the alienation of modernity to facile God-talk and recognizes modern culture's sense of autonomy and the principle that requires immanent meaning. This Enlightenment principle asserts that one cannot really accept something as true unless it shows itself to be so within human experience. It rejects an appeal to extrinsic authority on the face of it. No final commitment to ultimacy is possible that does not arise out of inner human exigency.[13] Is there any way of taking present-day culture seriously so that Christian spirituality need not simply hammer it with God's will? Can human experience itself suggest that the idea of God's will offers coherent meaning in our current world?

Three logical steps can preserve Calvin's conviction of the commanding relevance of God's will while completely transforming the way it makes its way into human consciousness. The first is to recognize that laws and the body of law do not merely consist of accumulated commands that regulate human behavior. The functions of the law that Calvin internalized are not sufficient for a humanist appropriation of law and legal tradition. Taking a larger view, law can be considered as embodying the set of values of a people and thus representing their culture. Like language itself, legal codes, no matter how they developed or are applied, bear witness to ideals that both express corporate experience and then shape it. The second step is to acknowledge a dimension of sacredness to these ideals. Such sacredness cannot easily be defined; it refers to a level of operation that communicates transcendence to value, where value refers to importance in and of itself. The "sacred" points to the quality of the value of human existence itself that is being protected by law—not this or that law but law itself. Sacrality points to transcendent value within the finite and secular. The third and final step occurs when one makes the connection between God and that sacredness. God enters into consciousness as the transcendent ground which supports and guarantees that the sacredness of human existence is real and not mere fancy. God subsists in but transcends the contingency of the evolutionary process. The value of the human person as absolute and sacred opens consciousness to the reality that grounds it.

This view can be tested. There are few if any people in the world who do not want justice when it comes to themselves: "I have my rights."[14] But it would be simply self-contradictory to claim rights for oneself and not affirm their relevance, precisely in equal measure, to others. What accounts for this demand and for its uncompromising universality? The question does not prove the existence of God, but God and God's will help make sense out of one of the deepest impulses of human existence and one of the basic questions humans address to themselves. These experiential underpinnings help people in today's scientifically nurtured secular culture to understand what Calvin and Barth are referring to with their bare biblical imperatives.

Intentional Use of Creatures

Finally, how do the broad questions of God and God's nature, of God's providence and God's will, come to bear on people's actual lives? How do these theological issues and ethical dilemmas enter into daily experience? Calvin asked these questions with his approach to the way one uses the creatures of this world in one's daily life. This question and Calvin's response to it apply directly to Christian spirituality. The issue shows how closely the disciplines of ethics and spirituality are related to each other and how general and abstract questions can suddenly gain traction on the road of Christian life.

The question of the use of the things of this world has a general and a specific dimension. Generally, one should use them as God intended them to be used. One examines their end, what they are for, and one goes with what one discerns to be the intended use that God has built into them through the mechanisms of evolution. The response bears the tone of classical ethical theory; it makes an appeal to teleology or God's purpose in creation. And Calvin's response seems open and reasonable: Whether it be for enjoyment or for practical necessity, creatures themselves define how they are to be used because they reflect the intentions of their creator.

On a more practical level of the particular decision, how should one go about deciding how to decide? Calvin counsels the use of reason and prudence in dealing with the world. He seems to apply the golden mean of Aristotle without using his name. Use in moderation, not excessively at either end, neither with rigidity nor laxity. In effect, he is counseling a reasonable or commonsensical approach to adjusting means to ends on the supposition that the creator God has built an ethical logic into creation itself. Once faith in God has entered the discernment process, reason is given full sway to interpret the constructive use of everyday gifts for how the Christian leads his or her life. Calvin does not surrender his evangelical perspective in these judgments. Rather, he shows that reason, whether it be philosophical or legal reasoning, does not compete with faithful thinking. In Calvin's case, the two are noncompetitively intertwined; each one operates within the other. Such counsel implies a sound and balanced estimate of the interacting influences between theology, ethics, and spiritual discernment.

To sum up, Calvin can communicate to the twenty-first century a balanced view of Christian spirituality or Christian life that integrates in a unique and explicit way the roles of theology and ethics. Very rarely has either his theology or his ethics departed sharply from what lies in the background: the life of the citizens of Geneva in the church of that city. This spirituality will need some adjustments in different historically conscious, socially mobile, urban, scientifically coherent, and pluralistic worlds. But these adjustments can be made. Calvin still provides a firm basis for Christian life.

Notes

1. Ordinarily a member of the church would think of himself or herself as a member of the elect, one chosen by God from eternity, one whom God's providence has provided and guided to this

particular moment in time. But the point here is not to legitimize Calvin's doctrine of predestination but to read the implications of his conception of God's sovereignty.

2. This experience, of course, originated within human consciousness in the first place and is carried within. But this describes the character of all doctrines because revelation takes place in human subjectivity.

3. In our day, it does not take much reflection to discredit Calvin's conceptions of God's wrath directed at God's creatures. It is one thing to imagine God's standing in judgment of sin that causes suffering, but God's will aims not at punishment but at overcoming sin and sinfulness. Debates about God's being torn between justice and love are simply wrong in their anthropomorphic premises. In the Bible, God as savior completely aligns with God as creator whether or not we can figure that out.

4. Ernst Troeltsch, *The Social Teaching of the Christian Churches* (New York: Harper Torchbooks, 1960), 617.

5. Calvin would not have accepted this interpretation; it was not within the ken of sixteenth-century Christianity. It is, rather, a twenty-first-century appropriation of the sovereignty of God as creator of heaven and earth.

6. The effect of an eschatological outlook in Calvin bears analogy with Luther's "freedom of the Christian" who stands in a new relationship with God on the basis of faith.

7. John H. Leith, *John Calvin's Doctrine of the Christian Life* (Louisville: Westminster/John Knox, 1989), 162–65.

8. This interpretation does not really contradict the meaning of John Cassian. The essential difference lies in the context; despite its autonomy, Geneva was not a monastery but a city-state related to other states and with the life of Europe coursing through its gates.

9. John D. Zizioulas, *Being as Communion: Studies in Personhood and the Church* (Crestwood, NY: St. Vladimir's Seminary Press, 1997), 174, n11.

10. Leith, *John Calvin's Doctrine of the Christian Life,* 165.

11. Calvin wrote that the office of ruler is a holy calling, "the most sacred and by far the most honorable of all callings in the whole life of mortal men" (4.20.4).

12. Troeltsch, *The Social Teachings,* 589.

13. See Maurice Blondel, *The Letter on Apologetics and History and Dogma*, ed. and trans. Alexander Dru and Illtyd Trethowan (New York: Holt, Rinehart and Winston, 1964), 156–61. This is not far from the logic implicit in the work of Friedrich Schleiermacher following the rationalism of the Enlightenment.

14. This universal sense is proven by the feeling of tragedy attached to persons who have lost their sense of self-worth.

Further Reading

Bruce, Gordon. *Calvin*. New Haven, CT: Yale University Press, 2009. [This comprehensive biography in narrative style features seminal scholarship from a Reformed scholar.]

Holder, R. Ward, ed. *John Calvin in Context*. Cambridge: Cambridge University Press, 2019. Online, 2020. [This small library on John Calvin from a historical perspective contains forty-nine short essays that describe the context of Calvin's birth, education, development, work, and influence.]

Kingdon, Robert M. "The Geneva Consistory in the Time of Calvin," *Calvinism in Europe: 1540–1620*, ed. Andrew Pettegree, Alastair Duke, and Gillian Lewis. New York: Cambridge University Press, 1994: 21–34; Idem., "The Institutional Matrix," *Adultery and Divorce in Calvin's Geneva*. Cambridge, MA: Harvard University Press, 1995: 7–30; Monter, E. William. "The Consistory of Geneva, 1559–1569," *Bibliothèque d'Humanisme et Renaissance* 38 (1976): 467–84. [These sources demythologize the place and role of the Consistory in Calvin's Geneva and provide practical insight into his spirituality.]

Leith, John H. *John Calvin's Doctrine of the Christian Life*. Louisville: Westminster/John Knox, 1989. ["The Christian Life" correlated neatly with the idea of spirituality, and this book brings out the social dimension of Calvin's conception of personal and social responsibility.]

McGrath, Alister E. *A Life of John Calvin: A Study in the Shaping of Western Culture*. Oxford: Basil Blackwell, 1990. [This is a relatively brief, sympathetic, and accessible life of Calvin that brings out the relevance of his theology for human life.]

McKee, Elsie Anne, ed. *John Calvin: Writings on Pastoral Piety* [Classics of Western Spirituality]. New York: Paulist Press, 2001. [This anthology, with a Preface by Brian A. Gerrish, provides texts that illustrate Calvin as a minister of the Christian gospel.]

McKim, Donald K. *The Cambridge Companion to John Calvin.* Cambridge: Cambridge University Press, 2006. [This edited compilation features essays on Calvin's preaching, biblical interpretation, piety, ethics, political conflicts, and approach to social issues.]

Mullett, Michael A. *John Calvin.* London: Routledge, 2011, 2016 online. [This life of Calvin locates him as a bridge between the late medieval and early modern world in Europe. It makes him a formative religious and cultural influence in the development of Western culture.]

Troeltsch, Ernst. *The Social Teaching of the Christian Churches.* New York: Harper Torchbooks, 1960. [This classic interpretation of John Calvin's theology and its influence on society in counterpoint to Luther situates in broad terms his relevance to Western culture.]

Watt, Jeffrey R. *The Consistory and Social Discipline in Calvin's Geneva.* Rochester: Rochester University Press, 2020 online. [This book reprises the function of the Consistory during Calvin's time in Geneva.]

About the Series

The volumes of this series provide readers direct access to important voices in the history of the faith. Each of the writings has been selected, first, for its value as a historical document that captures the cultural and theological expression of a figure's encounter with God. Second, as "classics," the primary materials witness to the "transcendent" in a way that has proved potent for the formation of Christian life and meaning beyond the particularities of the setting of its authorship.

Recent renewed interest in mysticism and spirituality have encouraged new movements, contributed to a growing body of therapeutic-moral literature, and inspired the recovery of ancient practices from Church tradition. However, the meaning of the notoriously slippery term "spirituality" remains contested. The many authors who write on the topic have different frameworks of reference, divergent criteria of evaluation, and competing senses of the principal sources or witnesses. This situation makes it important to state the operative definition used in this series. *Spirituality is the way people live in relation to what they consider to be ultimate.* So defined, spirituality is a universal phenomenon: everyone has one, whether they can fully articulate it or not. Spirituality emphasizes lived experience and concrete expression of one's principles, attitudes, and convictions, whether rooted in a defined tradition or not. It includes not only interiority and devotional practices but also the real outworkings of people's ideas and values. Students of spirituality examine the way that a person or group conceives of a meaningful existence through the practices that orient them toward their horizon of deepest meaning. What animates their life? What motivates their truest desires? What sustains them and instructs them? What provides for them a vision of the good life? How do they define and pursue truth? And how do they imagine and work to realize their shared vision of a good society?

The "classic" texts and authors presented in these volumes, though they represent the diversity of Christian traditions, define their ultimate value in God through Christ by the Spirit. They share a conviction that the Divine has revealed God's self in history through Jesus Christ. God's self-communication, in turn, invites a response through faith to participate in an intentional life of self-transcendence and to co-labor with the Spirit in manifesting the reign of God. Thus, *Christian spirituality refers to the way that individuals or social entities live out their encounter with God in Jesus Christ by a life in the Spirit.*

Christian spirituality necessarily involves a hermeneutical task. Followers of Christ set about the work of integrating knowledge and determining meaning through an interpretative process that refracts through different lenses: the life of Jesus, the witness of the scripture, the norms of the faith community, the traditions and social structures of one's heritage, the questions of direct experience, the criteria of the academy and other institutions that mediate truthfulness and viability, and personal conscience. These seemingly competing authorities can leave contemporary students of theology with more quandaries than clarity. Thus, this series has anticipated this challenge with an intentional structure that will guide students through their encounter with classic texts. Rather than providing commentary on the writings themselves, this series invites the audience to engage the texts with an informed sense of the context of their authorship and a dialog with the text that begins a conversation about how to make the text meaningful for theology, spirituality, and ethics in the present.

Most of the readers of these texts will be familiar with critical historical methods which enable an understanding of scripture in the context within which it was written. However, many people read scripture according to the common sense understanding of their ordinary language. This almost inevitably leads to some degree of misinterpretation. The Bible's content lies embedded in its cultural context, which is foreign to the experience of contemporary believers. Critical historical study enables a reader to get closer to an authentic past meaning by explicitly attending to the historical period, the situation of the author, and other particularities of the composition of the text. For example, one would miss the point of the story of the "Good Samaritan" if one did not recognize that the first-century Palestinian conflict between Jews and Samaritans makes the hero of the Jewish parable an enemy and an unlikely model of virtue! Something deeper than a simple offer of neighborly love is going on in this text.

However, the more exacting the critical historical method becomes, the greater it increases the distance between the text and the present-day reader. Thus, a second obstacle to interpreting classics for contemporary theology, ethics, and spirituality lies in a bias that texts embedded in a world so different from today cannot carry an inner authority for present life. How can we find something both true and relevant for faith today in a witness that a critical historical method determines to be in some measure alien? The basic problem has two dimensions: how do we appreciate the past witnesses of our tradition on their own terms, and, once we have, how can we learn from something so dissimilar?

Most Christians have some experience navigating this dilemma through biblical interpretation. Through Church membership, Christians have gained familiarity with scriptural language, and preaching consistently applies its content to daily life. But beyond the Bible, a long history of cultural understanding, linguistic innovation, doctrinal negotiations, and shifting patterns of practices has added layer upon layer of meaning to Christian spirituality. Veiled in unfamiliar grammar, images, and politics, these texts may appear as cultural artifacts suitable only for scholarly treatments. How can a modern student of theology understand a text cloaked in an unknown history and still encounter in it a transcendent faith that animates life in the present? Many historical and theological aspects of Christian spirituality that are still operative in communities of faith are losing traction among swathes of the population, especially younger generations. Their premises have been called into question; the metaphors are dead; the symbols appear unable to mediate grace; and the ideas appear untenable. For example, is the human species really saved by the blood of Jesus on the cross? What does it mean to be resurrected from the dead? How does the Spirit unify if the church is so divided? On the other hand, the positive experiences and insights that accrued over time and added depth to Christian spirituality are being lost because they lack critical appropriation for our time. For example, has asceticism been completely lost in present-day spirituality or can we find meaning for it today? Do the mystics live in another universe, or can we find mystical dimensions in religious consciousness today? Does monasticism bear meaning for those who live outside the walls?

This series addresses these questions with a three-fold strategy. The historical first step introduces the reader to individuals who represent key ideas, themes, movements, doctrinal developments, or remarkable distinctions in theology, ethics, or spirituality. This first section will equip readers with a sense of the context of the authorship and a grammar for understanding the text.

Second, the reader will encounter the witnesses in their own words. The selected excerpts from the authors' works have exercised great influence in the history of Christianity. Letting these texts speak for themselves will enable readers to encounter the wisdom and insight of these classics anew. Equipped with the necessary background and language from the introduction, students of theology will bring the questions and concerns of their world into contact with the world of the authors. This move personalizes the objective historical context and allows the existential character of the classic witness to appear. The goal is not the study of the exact meaning of ancient texts, as important as that is. That would require a task outside the scope of this series. Recommended readings will be provided for those who wish to continue digging into this important part of interpretation. These classic texts are not presented as comprehensive representations of their authors but as statements of basic characteristic ideas that still have bearing on lived experience of faith in the twenty-first century. The emphasis lies on existential depth of meaning rather than adequate representation of an historical period which can be supplemented by other sources.

Finally, each volume also offers a preliminary interpretation of the relevance of the author and text for the present. The methodical interpretations seek to preserve the past historical meanings while also bringing them forward in a way that is relevant to life in a technologically developed and pluralistic secular culture. Each retrieval looks for those aspects that can open realistic possibilities for viable spiritual meaning in current lived experience. In the unfolding wisdom of the many volumes, many distinct aspects of the Christian history of spirituality converge into a fuller, deeper, more far-reaching, and resonant language that shows what in our time has been taken for granted, needs adjustment, or has been lost (or should be). The series begins with fifteen volumes but, like Cassian's *Conferences*, the list may grow.

About the Editors

ROGER HAIGHT, a Visiting Professor at Union Theological Seminary in New York, has written several books in the area of fundamental theology. A graduate of the University of Chicago, he is a past president of the Catholic Theological Society of America.

ALFRED PACH III is an Associate Professor of Medical Sciences and Global Health at the Hackensack Meridian School of Medicine. He has a Ph.D. from the University of Wisconsin in Madison and an MDiv in Psychology and Religion from Union Theological Seminary.

AMANDA AVILA KAMINSKI is an Assistant Professor of Theology at Texas Lutheran University, where she also serves as Director of the Program in Social Innovation and Social Entrepreneurship. She has written extensively in the area of Christian spirituality.

Past Light on Present Life:
Theology, Ethics, and Spirituality

Roger Haight, SJ, Alfred Pach III,
and *Amanda Avila Kaminski,* series editors

Available titles:

Printed in the USA
CPSIA information can be obtained
at www.ICGtesting.com
JSHW020026020324
58416JS00002B/28